AN ADAPTED CLASSIC

W9-BAC-863

THE CALL OF
THE WILD

JACK LONDON

GLOBE BOOK COMPANY
A Division of Simon & Schuster
Englewood Cliffs, New Jersey

Cover design: Marek Antoniak
Cover illustration: Michael Garland
Interior illustrations: Den Schofield
Interior map: Andrea Vuocolo

ISBN: 0-83590-040-1

Printed in the United States of America
5 6 7 8 9 0

 GLOBE BOOK COMPANY
A Division of Simon & Schuster
Englewood Cliffs, New Jersey

ABOUT THE AUTHOR

Jack London was born in San Francisco, California, in 1876, and grew up in nearby Oakland. His family was poor when he was young, so that Jack had to quit school in his early teens and go to work. He worked as a newsboy, in a bowling alley, and in a factory. When he was 15, he was an oyster fisherman. Soon after that, he became a sailor, traveling as far as the Sea of Japan.

When he was 17, Jack London won a prize for an article about a storm at sea. That and other experiences made him decide to return to school. He completed high school in a year and entered the University of California. But he soon left the university and joined the Klondike gold rush to northern Canada.

When he returned from Canada, Jack London began to earn his living as a writer. He wrote large numbers of stories and articles, some of them based on his experiences at sea. Others, including *The Call of the Wild,* were based on his experiences in the far north. Published in 1903, when London was 27, *The Call of the Wild* quickly became popular and made London famous.

London devoted the rest of his life to writing and traveling. He also ran several times for public office as a socialist, but without success. Among his better known works are the novels *The Sea Wolf, White Fang,* and *Martin Eden,* and the short story "To Build a Fire." He died in 1916.

PREFACE

In the late 1890s, when the Klondike gold rush took place, the only way to get supplies into the far north in winter was by dogsled. Because of the great demand for sleds, there was a shortage of dogs to pull them. As a result, large dogs often were kidnapped from their homes in the United States and sent north to join the dog teams.

Buck was one of these dogs, and *The Call of the Wild* is his story. Taken from a comfortable life in California to a dog team, he learned to survive by "the law of club and fang." At the same time, the wild life of the forest called to him with ever greater force. The story of Buck's life is one of adventure, cruelty, and, finally, triumph.

ADAPTER'S NOTE

In preparing this edition of *The Call of the Wild,* we have kept closely to what Jack London wrote. We have modified some of London's vocabulary and simplified the structure of many of his sentences. Except for perhaps a half dozen sentences, however, nothing has been omitted.

CONTENTS

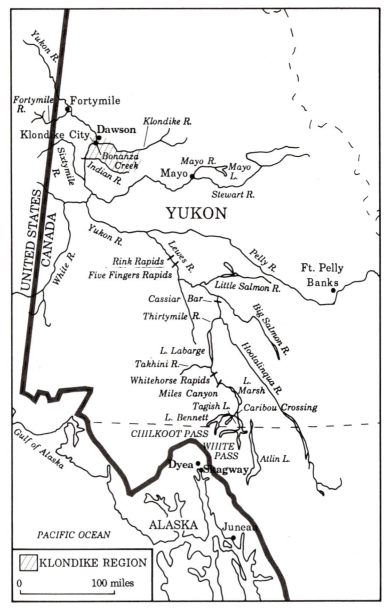

YUKON TERRITORY

1   *Into the Primitive*

Buck did not read the newspapers, or he would have known that trouble was brewing. It was brewing for every strong dog with warm, long hair on the Pacific coast, from Puget Sound to San Diego. Trouble was brewing because men, groping in the Arctic darkness, had found a yellow metal. Steamship and transportation companies were advertising the find, and thousands of men were rushing to the Northland. These men wanted dogs, and the dogs they wanted were heavy dogs, with strong muscles for working, and with furry coats to protect them from the frost.

Buck lived at a big house in the sun-kissed Santa Clara Valley. Judge Miller's Place, it was called. It stood back from the road, half hidden among the trees. Glimpses could be caught through the trees of the wide, cool veranda that ran around all four sides of the house. The house was approached by gravel driveways, which wound through wide lawns and under the connecting boughs of tall poplar trees. At the rear things were even more spacious than at the front. There were great stables, where a dozen grooms and boys worked. There were rows of vine-covered servants' cottages, an orderly cluster of small buildings, long grape arbors, green pastures, orchards, and berry patches. Then there was the pumping plant for the well, and the big cement tank where Judge Miller's boys took their morning swim and kept cool in the hot afternoon.

And over this great kingdom Buck ruled. Here he was born, and here he had lived the four years of his life. It was true, there were other dogs. There had to be other dogs on so vast a place, but they did not count. They came and went. Some of them lived in crowded kennels. Others lived unseen in the darkness of the house's inner rooms, like Toots, the Japanese pug, or Ysabel, the Mexican hairless—strange creatures that rarely put their noses out of doors or set their feet on the ground. On the other hand, there were the fox terriers, at least twenty of them. The terriers barked frightening promises at Toots and Ysabel, who looked out the windows at them, protected by a small army of housemaids with brooms and mops.

But Buck was neither a house dog nor a kennel dog. The whole kingdom was his. He plunged into the swimming tank or went hunting with the Judge's sons. He escorted Molly and Alice, the Judge's daughters, on long twilight or early-morning rambles. On wintry nights, he lay at the Judge's feet before the roaring fire in the house's library. He carried the Judge's grandsons on his back, or rolled them in the grass, and guarded them through wild adventures down to the fountain in the stable yard, and even beyond, where the paddocks and the berry patches were. He walked among the terriers in a stiff and haughty way, and Toots and Ysabel he totally ignored, for he was king—king over all creeping, crawling, flying things of Judge Miller's place, humans included.

His father, Elmo, a huge St. Bernard, had been the Judge's loyal companion, and Buck seemed likely to follow in his father's way. Buck was not so large—he weighed only 140 pounds—for his mother, Shep, had been a shepherd. Nevertheless, 140 pounds, along with a dignified manner that came from good living and widespread respect, enabled him to carry himself like a king. During the four years since his puppyhood he had lived the life of a stately nobleman. He was proud, even a bit arrogant, as country gentlemen sometimes become because of their isolation. But he had saved himself by not becoming merely a spoiled house dog. Hunting and other outdoor pleasures had kept down the fat and hardened his muscles; and his love of swimming had strengthened him and kept him healthy.

This was the kind of dog Buck was in the fall of 1897, when the Klondike strike dragged men from all the world into the frozen North. But Buck did not read the newspapers. Nor did he know that Manuel, one of the gardener's helpers, was a person that he should not trust. Manuel had one overpowering sin. He loved to play Chinese lottery. Also, in his gambling, he had one overpowering weakness—faith in a system; and this made his fate certain. For to play a system requires money, while the wages of a gardener's helper do not even cover the needs of a wife and several children.

On the night of Manuel's betrayal, the Judge was at a meeting of the Raisin Growers' Association, and the boys were busy organizing an athletic club. No one saw Manuel and Buck go off through the orchard. Buck thought they were just taking a walk. Except for one man, no one saw Manuel and Buck arrive at the little railroad station known as College Park. This man talked with Manuel, and money clinked between them.

"You might wrap up the goods before you deliver them," the stranger said gruffly. Manuel wound two loops of stout rope around Buck's neck under the collar.

"Twist it, and you'll choke him plenty," said Manuel. The stranger grunted in agreement.

Buck had accepted the rope with quiet dignity. To be sure, it was an action that he was not used to. But he had learned to trust in men that he knew, and to give them credit for greater wisdom than his own. He growled, however, when the ends of the rope were placed in the stranger's hands. He had merely hinted at his dislike, in his pride believing that a hint was all that was needed. But to his surprise, the rope tightened around his neck, shutting off his breath. In quick rage he sprang at the man, who met him halfway. The man grabbed him close by the throat, and with a quick twist threw him over on his back. Then the rope tightened without mercy. Buck struggled in a fury, his tongue hanging out of his mouth and his great chest panting helplessly. Never in all his life had he been so badly treated, and never in his life had he been so angry. But his strength drained away and his eyes grew glassy. By the time the train stopped and the two men threw him into the baggage car, he knew nothing.

The next he knew, he was dimly aware that his tongue was hurting and that he was being jolted along in some kind of car. The hoarse shriek of a locomotive whistle told him where he was. He had traveled too often with the Judge not to know the sensation of riding in a baggage car. He opened his eyes, and into them came the fury of a kidnapped king. The man sprang for Buck's throat, but Buck was too quick for him. His jaws closed on the hand. They did not relax until his senses were once more choked out of him.

"Yep, it has fits," the man said, hiding his badly wounded hand from the baggageman, who had been attracted by the sounds of struggle. "I'm taking him up to San Francisco for the boss. A top-notch dog doctor there thinks that he can cure him."

Later, in a little shed back of a saloon on the San Francisco waterfront, the man talked about that night's ride.

"All I get is fifty dollars," he grumbled. "I wouldn't do it again for a thousand dollars in cold cash."

His hand was wrapped in a bloody handkerchief, and the right trouser leg was ripped from knee to ankle.

"How much did the other punk get?" the saloonkeeper demanded.

"A hundred," was the reply, "He wouldn't take a cent less, so help me."

"That makes a hundred and fifty." the saloonkeeper added up. "He's worth it, or I'm a squarehead."

The kidnapper undid the bloody wrapping and looked at his injured hand. "If I don't get rabies——"

"It will be because you was born to hang," laughed the saloonkeeper. "Here, lend me a hand before you leave," he added.

Dazed, suffering unbearable pain from throat and tongue, with the life half choked out of him,

Buck tried to face his torturers. But he was thrown down and choked again and again, until the men at last finished filing the heavy brass collar from off his neck. Then the rope was removed, and he was thrown into a wooden crate that was like a cage.

There he lay for the rest of the weary night, nursing his anger and wounded pride. He could not understand what it all meant. What did these strange men want with him? Why were they keeping him caged in this narrow crate? He did not know why, but he felt weighed down by the uneasy sense that some disaster was about to happen. Several times during the night he sprang to his feet when the door rattled open. He expected to see the Judge, or at least the boys. But each time it was the saloon-keeper who looked in at him by the sickly light of a tallow candle. And each time the joyful bark that trembled in Buck's throat was twisted into a savage growl.

But the saloonkeeper let him alone, and in the morning four men entered and picked up the crate. More torturers, Buck decided. They were evil-looking men, ragged and scruffy. Buck stormed and raged at them through the bars, but they only laughed and poked sticks at him. He attacked the sticks with his teeth, until he realized that that was what they wanted. So he lay down sullenly and allowed the crate to be lifted into a wagon. Then he, and the crate in which he was caged, began a passage through many hands. Clerks in the express office took charge of him. He was carted about in another wagon. A truck carried him, with an assortment of boxes and packages, onto a ferry boat. He was trucked off the steamer into a great railway depot.

Finally, he was deposited in a railroad car.

For two days and nights this railroad car was dragged along at the tail of shrieking locomotives. For those two days and nights, Buck neither ate nor drank. In his anger he had met the first advances of the railroad workers with growls. They got back at him by teasing him. When he threw himself against the bars, shaking and foaming at the mouth, they laughed at him and teased him. They growled and barked like hateful dogs, mewed like cats, and flapped their arms and crowed like chickens. It was all very silly, he knew. But therefore it was all the more offensive to his dignity, and he grew more and more angry. He did not mind the hunger so much, but he suffered greatly from the lack of water, and he became even angrier. In fact, the ill treatment had thrown him into a fever, which was fed by the soreness of his thirsty and swollen throat and tongue.

He was glad for one thing: the rope was off his neck. That had given them an unfair advantage. Now that it was off, he would show them. He was determined that they would never get another rope around his neck. For two days and nights he neither ate nor drank. During those two days and nights of suffering, he built up so much rage that it looked very unsafe for the first person to get in his way. His eyes turned bloodshot, and he was transformed into a raging fiend. So changed was he that the Judge himself would not have recognized him. The railroad workers breathed with relief when they loaded him off the train at Seattle.

Four men carefully carried the crate from the wagon into a small, high-walled back yard. A stout man, with a red sweater that sagged at the neck, came out and signed the book for the driver. Buck guessed that this man was his next threat, and he hurled himself savagely against the bars. The man smiled grimly, and brought a hatchet and a club.

"You ain't going to take him out now?" the driver asked.

"Sure," the man replied, driving the hatchet into the crate to pry it open.

There was a rapid scattering of the four men who had carried in the crate. From safe perches on top of the wall, they got ready to watch the show.

Buck rushed at the splintering wood, sinking his teeth into it, wrestling with it. Wherever the hatchet fell on the outside, Buck was there on the inside, snarling and growling. The man in the red sweater was calmly determined to get him out, and Buck was just as furiously anxious to get out.

"Now, you red-eyed devil," he said, when he had made an opening big enough for Buck's body. At the same time he dropped the hatchet and shifted the club to his right hand.

And Buck was truly a red-eyed devil, as he drew himself together for the spring. His hair bristled, his mouth was foaming, and there was a mad glitter in his bloodshot eyes. Straight at the man he launched his 140 pounds of fury, with the built-up rage of two days and nights. Just as his jaws were about to close on the man, he received a shock that stopped his body in midair, and brought his teeth together with a painful jolt. He whirled over, hitting the ground on his back and side. He had never been struck by a club in his life, and he did not understand. With a snarl that was part bark and more scream, he was once again on his feet and launched into the air. And

again the shock came, and he was brought crashing to the ground. This time he was aware that it was the club, but he was too furious to be cautious. He charged a dozen times, and each time the club broke the charge and smashed him down.

After a particularly fierce blow, he crawled to his feet, too dazed to rush. He staggered limply about. Blood flowed from his nose and mouth and ears, and his beautiful coat was sprayed with bloody spit. Then the man advanced and deliberately dealt him a frightful blow on the nose. All the pain Buck had endured so far was nothing compared with the perfect agony of this. With a roar that was almost lionlike, he again hurled himself at the man. But the man, shifting the club from right to left, coolly caught him by the under jaw, at the same time jerking downward and backward. Buck turned a full circle in the air and half of another circle, then crashed to the ground on his head and chest.

For the last time he rushed. The man struck the shrewd blow he had purposely held back for so long. Buck crumpled up and went down, knocked completely senseless.

"He's no slouch at dog-breaking, that's what I say," one of the men on the wall cried enthusiastically.

"I'd rather break wild horses any day, and twice on Sundays," answered the driver, as he climbed on the wagon and started the horses.

Buck's senses came back to him, but not his strength. He lay where he had fallen, and from there he watched the man in the red sweater.

" 'Answers to the name of Buck,' " the man said to himself. He was quoting from the saloonkeeper's letter, which had announced the sending of the crate and dog. "Well, Buck, my boy," he went on in a friendly voice, "we've had our little excitement, and the best thing we can do is to let it go at that. You've learned your place, and I know mine. Be a good dog and all will go well. Be a bad dog, and I'll knock the stuffing out of you. Understand?"

As he spoke, he fearlessly patted the head of the dog that he had pounded so brutally. Although Buck's hair stiffened at the touch of the hand, he endured it without protest. When the man brought him water, he drank eagerly. Later he bolted a generous meal of raw meat, chunk by chunk, from the man's hand.

He was beaten. He knew that. But he was not broken. He saw, once for all, that he stood no chance against a man with a club. He had learned the lesson, and in all his after life he never forgot it. That club opened his eyes. It introduced him to the rule of primitive law, and he met the introduction halfway. The facts of life took on a fiercer appearance. Although he faced that fierceness without fear, he faced it with all the cunning of his nature aroused. As the days went by, other dogs came, in crates and at the end of ropes. Some came tamely, and some came raging and roaring as he had come. One and all, he watched them come under the control of the man in the red sweater. Again and again, as he looked at each brutal performance, the lesson was driven home to Buck: a man with a club was a lawgiver. He was a master to be obeyed, though not necessarily to act friendly toward. Of this last Buck was never guilty, though he did see beaten dogs that fawned upon the man, wagging their tails and licking his hand. Also he saw one dog that would neither act friendly nor obey. That dog finally was killed in the struggle for mastery.

Now and again men came, strangers, who talked to the man in the red sweater. Sometimes money passed between them, after which the strangers took one or more of the dogs away with them. Buck wondered where they went, for they never came back. But he was fearful of the future, and so he was glad each time when he was not selected.

Yet his time came, in the end, in the form of a little dried-up man. The man spat broken English and many strange and crude words that Buck could not understand.

"*Sacrédam!*" he cried, when his eyes lit upon Buck. "Dat one dam bully dog! Eh? How much?"

"Three hundred, and a present at that," promptly replied the man in the red sweater. "And since it's government money, you ain't got no kick coming, eh, Perrault?"

Perrault grinned. It was not an unfair sum for so fine an animal, considering that the price of dogs had been pushed sky-high by the great demand for them. The Canadian Government would not lose on the deal. Perrault knew dogs, and when he looked at Buck, he knew that he was one in a thousand. "One in ten thousand," he said to himself.

Buck saw money pass between them. He was not surprised when Curly, a good-natured Newfoundland dog, and he were led away by the little dried-up man. That was the last he saw of the man in the red sweater. As Curly and he looked at Seattle growing smaller from the deck of the *Narwhal*, it was the last he saw of the warm

Southland. Curly and he were taken below by Perrault and turned over to a giant called François. Perrault and François were French-Canadians. They were a new kind of man to Buck (of which he was destined to see many more). While he developed no warm feelings for them, he nonetheless grew honestly to respect them. He speedily learned that Perrault and François were fair men, calm and fair in administering justice, and too wise in the way of dogs to be fooled by dogs.

In the between decks of the *Narwhal,* Buck and Curly joined two other dogs. One of them was a big, snow-white fellow from Spitzbergen who had been brought away by a whaling captain, and who had later accompanied a Geological Survey into the Barrens. He was friendly but untrustworthy, smiling into one's face while he thought up some underhand trick. For instance, at the first meal he stole from Buck's food. As Buck sprang to punish him, François's whip sang through the air, reaching the thief first. Nothing remained for Buck to do but to recover the bone. That was fair of François, Buck decided, and François began his rise in Buck's judgment.

The other dog made no advances, nor did he receive any. Also, he did not attempt to steal from the newcomers. He was a gloomy, brooding fellow, and he showed Curly plainly that all he wanted was to be left alone, and further, that there would be trouble if he were not left alone. He was called Dave, and he ate and slept, or yawned between times, and took interest in nothing. He was not interested even when the *Narwhal* crossed Queen Charlotte Sound and rolled and pitched and bucked like a thing possessed. Buck and Curly grew excited, half wild with fear. But Dave raised his head as though annoyed, glanced casually at them, yawned, and went to sleep again.

Day and night the ship throbbed to the tireless pulse of the propeller. Though one day was very like another, Buck could tell that the weather was steadily growing colder. At last, one morning, the propeller was quiet, and the *Narwhal* took on an air of excitement. He felt it, as did the other dogs, and knew that a change was at hand. François leashed them and brought them on deck. At the first step upon the cold surface, Buck's feet sank into a white mushy something very much like mud. He sprang back with a snort. More of the white stuff was falling through the air. He shook himself, but more of it fell upon him. He sniffed it curiously, then licked some on his tongue. It bit like fire, and the next instant was gone. This puzzled him. He tried it again, with the same result. The onlookers laughed noisily, and he felt ashamed, he knew not why, for it was his first snow.

The Law of Club and Fang

Buck's first day on the Dyea beach was like a nightmare. Every hour was filled with shock and surprise. He had been suddenly jerked from the heart of civilization and flung into the heart of a primitive world. This was not a lazy, sun-kissed life, with nothing to do but loaf and be bored. There was neither peace here, nor rest, nor a moment's safety. Everything was confusion and action, and life and limb were in danger at every moment. There was an absolute need to be always alert, for these dogs and men were not town dogs and men. They were savages, all of them. The only law they knew was the law of club and fang.

He had never seen dogs fight the way these wolfish creatures fought. His first experience taught him an unforgettable lesson. It was a secondhand experience, to be sure, or he would not have lived to profit by it. Curly was the victim. They were camped near the log store where she, in her friendly way, made advances to a husky dog the size of a full-grown wolf, though not half so large as she. There was no warning, only a leap like a flash, a metallic clip of teeth, and an equally swift backward leap. Curly's face was ripped open from eye to jaw.

It was the wolf manner of fighting, to strike and leap away. But there was more to it than this. Thirty or forty huskies ran to the spot and surrounded the fighters in an intent and silent circle. Buck did not understand that silent intentness, nor the eager way with which they were licking their chops. Curly rushed her attacker, who struck again and leaped aside. He met her next rush with his chest, in a way that tumbled her off her feet. She never got up again. This was what the onlooking huskies had waited for. They closed in on her, snarling and yelping, and she was buried, screaming with agony, beneath the raging mass of bodies.

It was so sudden, and so unexpected, that Buck was startled. He saw Spitz run out his bright red tongue in the way he had of laughing. He saw François, swinging an axe, spring into the mess of dogs. Three men with clubs were helping him to scatter them. It did not take long. Two minutes from the time that Curly went down, the last of her attackers were clubbed off. But she lay there limp and lifeless in the bloody, trampled snow, almost literally torn to pieces, with François standing over her and cursing horribly. The scene often came back to Buck to trouble him in his sleep. So that was the way. No fair play. Once down, that was the end of you. Well, he would see to it that he never went down. Spitz ran out his tongue and laughed again, and from that moment Buck hated him with a bitter and deathless hatred.

Before he had recovered from the shock caused by the horrible death of Curly, he received another shock. François put an arrangement of straps and buckles on him. It was a harness, such as he had seen the grooms put on the horses at home. And as he had seen horses work, so he was put to work. He hauled François on a sled to the forest at the edge of the valley, and they returned with a load of firewood. Though his pride was hurt by having to be a draft animal, he was too wise to rebel. He buckled down with a will and did his best, though it was all new and strange. François was stern. He demanded to be obeyed instantly, and by virtue of his whip he was obeyed instantly. Dave, who was an experienced wheeler, nipped Buck's hind quarters whenever he made a mistake. Spitz, the leader, was also experienced. While he could not always get at Buck, he growled sharply from time to time, or he would cunningly throw his weight in the traces to jerk Buck into the way he should go. Buck learned easily, and under the combined teaching of his two mates and François, he made remarkable progress. Before they returned to camp he knew enough to stop at "ho," to go ahead at "mush," to swing wide on the turns, and to keep clear of the wheeler when the loaded sled shot downhill at their heels.

"Three very good dogs," François told Perrault. "Dat Buck, him pull like hell. I teach him quick as anything."

By afternoon Perrault, who was in a hurry to be on the trail with his dispatches, returned with two more dogs. He called them Billee and Joe. They were brothers, and both were true huskies. Although they were sons of one mother, they were as different as day and night. Billee's one fault was being too good natured. Joe was the very opposite, sour and brooding, with a constant snarl and a sinister eye. Buck received them in a comradely way, Dave ignored them, while Spitz proceeded to clobber first one and then the other. Billee wagged his tail, turned to run when he saw that giving in was of no avail, and cried (still giving in) when Spitz's sharp teeth scored his flank. But no matter how Spitz circled, Joe whirled around on his heels to face him, mane bristling, ears laid back, lips snarling, jaws clipping together as fast as he could snap, and eyes fiendishly gleaming—the embodiment of fear fighting back. His appearance was so terrible that Spitz was forced to give up disciplining him. But to cover his own embarrassment he turned upon the harmless and wailing Billee and drove him to the edge of the camp.

By evening Perrault obtained another dog, an old husky, long and lean and gaunt. His face was battle-scarred, and his single eye flashed a warning in a way that commanded respect. He was called Sol-leks, which means The Angry One. Like Dave, he asked nothing, gave nothing, expected nothing. When he marched slowly and unhurriedly into their midst, even Spitz left him alone. He had one quirk, which Buck was unlucky enough to discover. He did not like to be approached on his blind side. Buck was unintentionally guilty of this offense. The first knowledge he had of his mistake was when Sol-leks whirled on him and slashed his shoulder to the bone for three inches up and down. Forever after Buck avoided his blind side, and to the last of their comradeship had no more trouble. His only apparent ambition, like Dave's, was to be left alone. Buck was afterward to learn, though, that each of them possessed one other and even more vital ambition.

That night Buck faced the great problem of sleeping. The tent, lit by a candle, glowed warmly in the middle of the white plain. Buck, as a matter of course, entered the tent. But Perrault and François

cursed him and threw cooking utensils at him until he recovered from his fright and fled, humiliated, into the outer cold. A chill wind was blowing that nipped him sharply and bit with special sharpness into his wounded shoulder. He lay down on the snow and tried to sleep, but the frost soon drove him shivering to his feet. Miserable and depressed, he wandered about among the many tents, only to find that one place was as cold as another. Here and there savage dogs rushed upon him, but he bristled his neck hair and snarled (for he was learning fast), and they let him go his way unharmed.

Finally an idea came to him. He would return and see how his own teammates were making out. To his amazement, they had disappeared. Again he wandered about through the great camp, looking for them, and again he returned. Were they in the tent? No, that could not be, or he would not have been driven out. Then where could they possibly be? With drooping tail and shivering body, very forlorn indeed, he aimlessly circled the tent. Suddenly the snow gave way beneath his front legs, and he sank down. Something was wriggling under his feet. He sprang back, bristling and snarling, fearful or the unseen and unknown. But a friendly little yelp reassured him, and he went back to investigate. A whiff of warm air rose up to his nostrils, and there, curled up under the snow in a snug ball, lay Billee. He whined in a friendly way and wriggled to show his good will. As a bribe for peace, he even licked Buck's face with his warm, wet tongue.

Another lesson. So that was the way they did it. Buck confidently selected a spot, and with much fuss and waste effort dug a hole for himself. In an instant the heat from his body filled the narrow space, and he was asleep. The day had been long and hard, and he slept soundly and comfortably, though he growled and barked and wrestled with bad dreams.

Nor did he open his eyes until he was wakened by the noises of the waking camp. At first he did not know where he was. It had snowed during the night, and he was completely buried. The snow walls pressed him on every side, and a great surge of fear swept through him. It was the fear of the wild thing for the trap. The fear was a sign that he was returning through his own life to the lives of his ancestors; for he was a civilized dog who had had no experience of traps in his own life. The muscles of his whole body contracted, and the hair on his neck and shoulders stood on end. With a ferocious snarl he bounded straight up into the blinding day, the snow flying about him in a flashing cloud. Even before he landed on his feet, he saw the white camp spread out before him. He knew where he was, and he remembered everything that had happened from the time he went for a stroll with Manuel to the hole he had dug for himself the night before.

François shouted when Buck appeared. "What I say?" the dog driver called to Perrault. "That Buck for sure learn quick as anything."

Perrault nodded gravely. As courier for the Canadian Government, carrying important documents, he was anxious to obtain the best dogs. He was particularly pleased to have Buck.

Within an hour, three more huskies were added to the team. Before another quarter of an hour had passed, they were in harness and swinging up the trail toward the Dyea Canyon. Buck was glad to be gone. The work was hard, but he found that he did not dislike it. He was surprised at the whole team's eagerness. Still more surprising was the change in Dave and Sol-leks. They were new dogs, completely changed by putting on a harness. Gone was their lack of energy and interest. They were now alert and active, eager that the work should go well, and impatient with anything that held that work back. Working in the traces seemed to be their main way of expressing themselves. It was what they lived for and the only thing they took delight in.

Dave was the wheeler or sled dog. Pulling in front of him was Buck. In front of Buck was Sol-leks. The rest of the team was strung out ahead, single file, to the leader, which position was filled by Spitz.

Buck had been purposely placed between Dave and Sol-leks so that he might receive instruction. Buck was a good student, and Dave and Sol-leks were equally good teachers. They never allowed him to make a mistake for long, enforcing their teaching with their sharp teeth. Dave was fair and very wise. He never nipped Buck without a reason, and he never failed to nip him when he needed it. François's whip backed him up, and Buck learned that it was cheaper to change his ways than to try to get revenge. Once, during a brief halt, when he got tangled in the traces and delayed the start, both Dave and Sol-leks flew at him and gave him a sound trouncing. The tangle that resulted was even worse, but after that Buck took good care to keep the traces clear. Before the day was over, he had mastered his work so well that his partners almost stopped nagging him. François's whip snapped less often, and Perrault even honored Buck by lifting up his feet and carefully examining them.

It was a hard day's run, up the Canyon, through the Sheep Camp, past the Scales and the timber line, and across glaciers and snowdrifts hundreds of feet deep. They crossed the great Chilkoot Divide, which stands between the salt water and the fresh water and guards forbiddingly the sad and lonely North. They made good time down the chain of lakes that fill the craters of extinct volcanoes. Late that night they pulled into the huge camp at the head of Lake Bennett, where thousands of gold seekers were building boats in preparation for the break-up of the ice in the spring. Buck made his hole in the snow and slept the sleep of the exhausted. All too early he was wakened in the cold darkness and harnessed with his mates to the sled.

That day they made forty miles, because the snow in the trail was already packed down. But the next day, and for many days after, they broke their own trail, worked harder, and made poorer time. Perrault usually traveled ahead of the team, packing the snow with snowshoes to make it easier for them. François, guiding the sled at the gee pole, sometimes changed places with him, but not often. Perrault was in a hurry, and he prided himself on his knowledge of ice. This knowledge was absolutely necessary, for the autumn ice was very thin, and where there was swift water, there was no ice at all.

Day after day, Buck toiled in the traces. They always broke camp in the dark, and the first gray of dawn found them hitting the trail with miles already traveled behind them. And they always pitched camp after dark, eating their bit of fish, and crawling to sleep in the snow. Buck was hungrier than he had ever been. The pound and a half of sun-dried salmon, which was his ration for each day, seemed to go nowhere. He never had enough, and suffered from constant pangs of hunger. Yet the other dogs, because they weighed less and were born to the life, received only a pound of the fish and managed to keep in good condition.

He quickly gave up the careful ways that had characterized his old life. A dainty eater, he found that his mates, finishing first, robbed him of his uneaten portion. There was no way to protect it. While he was fighting off two or three, it was disappearing down the throats of the others. To prevent this, he ate as fast as they did, and still he was so hungry that he was not above taking from others. He watched and learned. Once he saw Pike, a new dog who was a clever loafer and a thief, slyly steal a slice of bacon when Perrault's back was turned. Buck repeated the performance the following day, getting away with the whole chunk. A great uproar was raised, but Buck was not suspected. Instead Dub, an awkward blunderer who was always getting caught, was punished for Buck's stealing.

This first theft showed that Buck was able to succeed in the unfriendly Northland environment. It showed his ability to adjust to changing conditions. Without this ability, death would have been swift and terrible. It also marked the decay of his moral nature, which would have been a handicap in the ruthless struggle to survive. It was all well enough in the Southland, under the law of love and fellowship, to respect private property and personal feelings. But in the Northland, under the law of club and fang, whoever took such things into account was a fool who would fail to do well.

Not that Buck reasoned it out. He was fit, that was all, and without thinking about it, he adjusted himself to the new mode of life. All his days, no matter what the odds, he had never run from a fight. But the club of the man in the red sweater had beaten into him a more basic and primitive rule. When he was civilized, he could have died for a moral reason, such as, for example, protecting Judge Miller's riding whip. His ability to turn away from moral thinking, and so save his hide, showed that he now had left civilization completely behind. He did not steal for joy of it, but because of his hunger. He did not rob openly, but stole secretly and cunningly, out of respect for club and fang. In short, he did what he did because it was easier to do it than not to do it.

His development (or backsliding) was rapid. His muscles became hard as iron, and he grew uncaring about all ordinary pain. He could eat anything, no matter how revolting. Once eaten, the juices of his stomach extracted every last particle of nutrition. His blood carried it to the farthest reaches of his body, building it into the toughest of muscles. Sight and scent became remarkable. His hearing became so acute that in his sleep he heard the faintest sound and knew whether it meant peace or danger. He learned to bite the ice out with his teeth when it collected between his toes. When he was thirsty and there was ice over the water hole, he would break it by rearing and striking it with stiff front legs. His most striking trait was an ability to scent the wind and predict its direction a night in advance. No matter how still the air when he dug his nest by tree or bank, the wind that later blew found him on the side away from the wind, sheltered and snug.

And not only did he learn by experience, but instincts long dead became alive again. The tamed generations of his ancestors fell from him. In vague ways he remembered back to when the breed was young, to the time when wild dogs ranged in packs through the prehistoric forest and killed their meat as they ran it down. It was no task for him to learn to fight with cut and slash and the quick wolf snap. His ancestors had fought in this manner. The old tricks that they had stamped into the heredity of the breed were his tricks. They came to him without effort or discovery, as though they had always been his. And when, on the still, cold nights, he pointed his nose at a star and howled long and wolflike, it was his ancestors who were howling down through the centuries and through him. And his howls were their howls, the howls that voiced the meaning to them of the stillness, and the cold, and the dark.

Thus the ancient song surged through him, and he came into his own again. And this happened because men had found a yellow metal in the North, and because Manuel was a gardener's helper whose wages did not meet the needs of his wife and several children.

3 The Primitive Beast

The primitive beast was strong in Buck, and under the fierce conditions of trail life it grew and grew. Yet it was a secret growth. He was too busy adjusting himself to the new life to feel at ease. Not only did he not pick fights, he avoided them whenever possible. There was a kind of careful thoroughness in his attitude. He was not prone to recklessness and sudden action. In the bitter hatred between him and Spitz, he showed no impatience and avoided all quarrelsome acts.

On the other hand, possibly because he saw Buck as a dangerous rival, Spitz never lost an opportunity to show his teeth. He even went out of his way to bully Buck. He tried constantly to start a fight, a fight that could end only in the death of one dog or the other. Early in the trip this might have taken place had it not been for an unusual accident. At the end of this day, they made a bleak and miserable camp on the shore of Lake Labarge. Driving snow, a wind that cut like a white-hot knife, and darkness had forced them to grope for a camping place. They could hardly have done worse. At their backs rose a wall of rock. Perrault and François were forced to make their fire and spread their sleeping robes on the ice of the lake itself. They had discarded their tent at Dyea in order to travel light. They built a fire of a few sticks of driftwood, but the fire melted through the ice and left them to eat supper in the dark.

Buck made his nest close to the sheltering rock. It was so snug and warm that he was reluctant to leave it when François passed out the fish, which he had thawed over the fire. But when Buck finished his share and returned, he found his nest occupied. A warning snarl told him that the intruder was Spitz. Until now Buck had avoided trouble with his enemy, but this was too much. The beast in him roared. He sprang on Spitz with a fury that surprised them both, but especially Spitz. Spitz's whole experience with Buck had taught him that Buck was an unusually timid dog, one who held his own only because of his great weight and size.

François was surprised, too, when they shot out in a tangle from the disrupted nest and he realized the cause of the trouble. "A-a-ah!" he cried to Buck. "Give it to him, by Gar! Give it to him, the dirty thief!"

Spitz was equally willing. He was crying with sheer rage and eagerness as he circled back and forth for a chance to spring in. Buck was no less eager, and no less cautious, as he likewise circled back and forth for the advantage. But it was then that the unexpected thing happened, the thing that put off their struggle for supremacy far into the future.

An oath from Perrault, the resounding impact of a club upon a bony frame, and a shrill yelp of pain were the first signals of a period of noise and confusion. The camp was suddenly discovered to be alive with starving huskies, eighty or a hundred of them, who had scented the camp from some Indian village.

They had crept in while Buck and Spitz were fighting. When the two men sprang among them with heavy clubs, they showed their teeth and fought back. The smell of the food made them crazy. Perrault found one with his head buried in the food box. His club landed heavily on the gaunt ribs, and the box was tipped over on the ground. Instantly there were twenty hungry animals scrambling for the bread and bacon. They ignored the blows of the clubs. They yelped and howled under the rain of blows, but struggled madly until the last crumb had been eaten.

In the meantime the astonished team dogs had burst out of their nests, only to be attacked by the fierce invaders. Never had Buck seen such dogs. It seemed as though their bones would burst through their skins. They were mere skeletons, their skins hanging loosely on their frames, with blazing eyes and drooling fangs. But the hunger madness made them powerful and terrifying. The team dogs were swept back against the cliff at the first attack. Buck was attacked by three huskies, and in an instant his head and shoulders were ripped and slashed. The uproar was frightening. Billee was crying as usual. Dave and Sol-leks, dripping blood from a dozen wounds, were fighting bravely side by side. Joe was snapping like a demon. Once his teeth closed on the front leg of a husky, and he crunched down through the bone. Pike leaped upon the crippled animal, breaking its neck with a quick flash of teeth and a jerk. Buck got a frothing enemy by the throat, and was sprayed with blood when his teeth sank through the jugular vein. The warm taste of it in his mouth urged him on to greater fierceness. He threw himself onto another husky, and at the same time he felt teeth sink into his own throat. It was Spitz, treacherously attacking from the side.

Perrault and François had cleaned out their part of the camp and now hurried to save their sled dogs. The wild wave of starving animals rolled back before them, and Buck shook himself free. But it was only for a moment. The two men had to run back to save the food, and the huskies returned to the attack. Billee, terrified into bravery, sprang through the savage circle and fled away over the ice. Pike and Dub followed on his heels, with the rest of the team behind. As Buck drew himself together to spring after them, out of the corner of his eye he saw Spitz rush toward him, apparently intending to throw him down. Once off his feet and under that mass of huskies, there was no hope for him. But he braced himself to the shock of Spitz's charge, then joined the flight out on the lake.

Later, the nine team dogs gathered together and looked for shelter in the forest. Although they had not been chased, they were in a bad way. Each of them was wounded in at least four or five places, and some were wounded severely. Dub was badly injured in a hind leg. Dolly, the last husky added to the team at Dyea, had a badly torn throat. Joe had lost an eye. And Billee, the good-natured, with an ear chewed to ribbons, cried and whimpered throughout the night. At daybreak they limped cautiously back to camp, where they found the looters gone and the two men in bad tempers. Fully half their food supply was gone. The huskies had chewed through the sled straps and canvas coverings. In fact, nothing that might possibly be eaten had escaped them. They had eaten a pair of Perrault's moose-hide moccasins, chunks out of the leather straps, and even two feet from the end of François's whip. He broke from his gloomy thoughts about the whip to look over his wounded dogs.

"Ah, my friends," he said softly, "maybe it make you mad dog, those many bites. Maybe all mad dog. *Sacrédam!* What you think, eh, Perrault?"

The courier shook his head doubtfully. With 400 miles of trail still between him and Dawson, he could not afford to have rabies break out among his dogs. Two hours of cursing and hard work got the harnesses into shape, and the wound-stiffened team was under way. They struggled painfully over the hardest part of the trail they had seen so far (and for that matter, the hardest part of the entire trail).

The Thirty Mile River was wide open. Its wild water did not want to freeze, and it was only in the eddies and in the quiet places that the ice held at all. Six days of exhausting effort were needed to cover those thirty terrible miles. And terrible they were, for the lives of dogs and men were at risk every foot of the way. Perrault, who was nosing the way, broke through the ice bridges a dozen times. He was saved each time by the long pole he carried, which he held so that it fell across the hole made by his body. But a cold snap was on, the thermometer registering fifty degrees below zero. Each time Perrault broke through the ice, he had to build a fire and dry his garments, or else he would freeze to death.

Nothing frightened or discouraged him. It was because nothing frightened or discouraged him that he had been chosen to be a government courier. He took all kinds of risks, single-mindedly pushing his little pinched face into the frost and struggling on from dim dawn to dark. He skirted the shores on rim ice that bent and crackled under foot, and on which they dared not stop. Once the sled broke through the ice, along with Dave and Buck. They were half-frozen and all but drowned by the time they were dragged out. As usual, a fire had to be built to save them from freezing. They were solidly coated with ice. The two men kept them running around the fire, sweating and thawing, coming so close to the fire that they were singed by the flames.

Another time Spitz went through, dragging the whole team after him up to Buck. Buck pulled backward with all his strength, his front paws on the slippery edge and the ice trembling and snapping all around. But behind him was Dave, who also was straining backward, and behind the sled was François, pulling till his tendons cracked.

Again, the rim ice broke away before and behind, and there was no escape except up the cliff. Perrault scaled it by a miracle, while François prayed for just that miracle. With every sled lashing and bit of harness made into a long rope, the dogs were hoisted, one by one, to the top of the cliff. François came up last, after the sled and its load. Then came the search for a place to descend. The descent eventually was made using the rope, and by nightfall they were back on the river a quarter of a mile from where they had started.

By the time they reached the Hootalinqua and good ice, Buck was worn out. The rest of the dogs were in the same condition, but Perrault pushed them to make up lost time. The first day they covered thirty-five miles to the Big Salmon. The next day saw thirty-five more to the Little Salmon. The third day they covered forty miles, which brought them well up toward the Five Fingers.

Buck's feet were not so compact and hard as the feet of the huskies. His feet had softened during the many generations since the day his last wild ancestor was tamed by a cave dweller. All day long he limped in agony. Once camp was made, he lay down like a dead dog. Hungry though he was, he would not move to receive his ration of fish, which François had to bring to him. The dog driver also rubbed Buck's feet for half an hour each night after supper, and he gave up the tops of his own moccasins to make four moccasins for Buck. This was a great relief. One morning Buck caused even the withered face of Perrault to twist itself into a grin. François had forgotten the moccasins, and Buck lay on his back, his four feet waving in the air, and refused to budge without them. Later his feet grew hard to the trail, and the worn-out footgear was thrown away.

At the Pelly one morning, as they were harnessing up, Dolly, who had never stood out in any way, suddenly went mad. She announced her condition by a long, heartbreaking wolf howl that sent every dog bristling with fear. Then she sprang straight for Buck. He had never seen a dog go mad, and he had no reason to fear madness. But he knew that here was horror, and he fled from it in a panic. He raced straight away, with Dolly, panting and frothing, one leap behind. She could not gain on him, because his terror was so great. But he could not pull away from her, because her madness was so great. He plunged through the wooded part of the island, flew down to the lower end, crossed a back channel filled with ice to another island, curved back to the main river, and in desperation started to cross it. All the time, though he did not look, he could hear her snarling just one step behind. François called to him a quarter of a mile away and he doubled back, still one leap ahead, gasping painfully for air. He put all his faith in the idea that François would save him. The dog driver held the axe ready in his hand, and as Buck shot past him, the axe crashed down on mad Dolly's head.

Buck staggered over against the sled, exhausted, sobbing for breath, and helpless. This was Spitz's opportunity. He sprang on Buck, and twice his teeth sank into his unresisting enemy, ripping and tearing the flesh to the bone. Then François's lash came down. Buck had the satisfaction of watching Spitz receive the worst whipping yet given to any of the team.

"One devil, dat Spitz," remarked Perrault. "Some day him kill dat Buck."

"Dat Buck two devils," François replied. "All de time I watch dat Buck, I know for sure. Listen: some fine day him get mad like hell and den him chew dat Spitz all up and spit him out on de snow. Sure. I know."

From then on, it was war between them. Spitz, as lead dog and recognized master of the team, felt his position threatened by this strange Southland dog. And Buck was strange to him, for of the many Southland dogs he had known, not one had done well in camp and on the trail. They were all too soft, dying under the hard work, the cold, and the starvation. Buck was the exception. He alone survived and did well, matching the husky in strength, savagery, and cunning. He was a masterful dog. He was dangerous because the club of the man in the red sweater had knocked all blind bravery and recklessness out of his desire for mastery. He was supremely cunning, and could bide his time.

It was unavoidable that the clash for leadership should come. Buck wanted it. He wanted it because it was his nature, because he had been gripped tight by that nameless, mysterious pride of the trail. It was a pride that kept dogs working to the last gasp, that lured them to die joyfully in the harness, and that broke their hearts if they were cut out of the harness. This was the pride of Dave as wheel dog and of Sol-leks as he pulled with all his strength. It was the pride that laid hold of them at break of camp, transforming them from sour and sullen brutes into straining, eager, ambitious creatures. It was the pride that spurred them on all day and dropped them at pitch of camp at night, letting them fall back into gloomy unrest and discontent. This was the pride that bore up Spitz. It made him thrash the sled dogs who made mistakes and didn't pull their weight, or who hid at harness-up time in the morning. Likewise it was this pride that made him fear Buck as a possible lead dog. And this was Buck's pride, too.

He openly threatened the other's leadership. He came between him and the shirkers he should have punished. And he did it on purpose. One night there was a heavy snowfall, and in the morning, Pike, the avoider of work, did not appear. He was securely hidden in his nest under a foot of snow. François called and looked for him in without success. Spitz was wild with anger. He raged through the camp, smelling and digging in every likely place, snarling so fright-fully that Pike heard and shivered in his hiding place.

But when he was at last unearthed, and Spitz flew at him to punish him, Buck flew, with equal rage, in between. It was so unexpected, and so clev-erly managed, that Spitz was hurled backward and off his feet. Pike, who had been trembling in fear, took heart at this open rebellion and sprang on his overthrown leader. Buck, who had forgotten the idea of fair play, likewise sprang on Spitz. François chuck-led at the incident. But it was his job to see that jus-tice was done, and so he brought his whip down on Buck with all his might. This failed to drive Buck from his fallen rival, and the butt of the whip was brought into play. Half-stunned by the blow, Buck was knocked backward, and the whip hit him again and again. Meanwhile, Spitz soundly punished Pike.

In the days that followed, as Dawson grew closer and closer, Buck continued to interfere between Spitz and the offenders. But he did it shrewdly, when François was not around. With the secret mutiny of Buck, a general disobedience sprang up and increased. Dave and Sol-leks were unaffected, but the rest of the team went from bad to worse. Things no longer went right. There was continual quarrel-ing. Trouble was always afoot, and Buck was at the bottom of it. He kept François busy, for the dog driv-er feared the coming life-and-death struggle between the two dogs, which he knew must take place sooner or later. On more than one night, the sounds of quar-reling and conflict among the other dogs turned him out of his sleeping robe, fearful that Buck and Spitz were at it.

But the opportunity did not come, and they pulled into Dawson one dreary afternoon with the great fight still to come. Here were many men and countless dogs, and Buck found them all at work. It seemed that all dogs worked here. All day they swung up and down the main street in long teams, and in the night, their jingling bells still went by. They hauled cabin logs and firewood, carried freight up to the mines, and did all kinds of work that horses did in the Santa Clara Valley. Here and there Buck met Southland dogs, but most dogs were the wild wolf husky breed. Regularly every night, at nine, twelve, and three, they lifted a nighttime song, a weird and eerie chant, which Buck delighted to join.

With the northern lights flaming coldly overhead, or the stars leaping in the frost dance, and the land numb and frozen under its carpet of snow, this song was filled with the sorrow of uncounted generations. When Buck moaned and sobbed the song, it was with the pain of living that was the pain of his wild fathers, and with the feelings of fear and mystery they had for the cold and dark.

Seven days from the time they pulled into Dawson, they dropped down a steep bank to the Yukon Trail, and pulled out for Dyea and Salt Water. Perrault was carrying dispatches even more urgent than those he had brought in. Also, he had decided to try to make the trip in record time for the year. Several things favored him in this. The week's rest had allowed the dogs to recover and had put them in good shape. The trail they had broken was now packed hard by later travelers. And further, the police had arranged to leave deposits of food in two or three places along the route, and so he could travel light.

They made Sixty Mile, which is a fifty-mile run, on the first day. The second day saw them booming up the Yukon well on their way to Pelly. But such splendid running was achieved only with great trouble and irritation for François. The sly revolt led by Buck had wrecked the unity of the team. It no longer was like one dog leaping in the traces. Buck's encouragement led the rebels into all kinds of petty crimes. No more was Spitz a leader greatly to be feared. The old respect departed, and they felt strong enough to challenge him. Pike robbed him of half a fish one night, and gulped it down under the protection of Buck. Another night Dub and Joe fought Spitz and made him hold back the punishment they deserved. And even Billee, the good-natured, was less good-natured, and whined not half so humbly as in former days. Buck never came near Spitz without snarling and bristling threateningly. In fact, he behaved very much like a bully, and he was given to strutting up and down before Spitz's very nose.

The breakdown of discipline also affected the dogs in their relations with one another. They quarreled more than ever among themselves, until at times the camp was a howling madhouse. Dave and Sol-leks alone were unchanged, though they were annoyed by the unending squabbling. François swore strange, wild oaths, and stamped the snow in useless rage, and tore his hair. His whip was always whistling among the dogs, but it did little good. As soon as his back was turned, the dogs were at it again. He backed up Spitz with his whip, while Buck backed up the rest of the team. François knew that

Buck was behind all the trouble, and Buck knew that he knew. But Buck was too clever ever to be caught red-handed again. He worked faithfully in the harness, for the labor had become a delight to him. Yet it was a greater delight to slyly start a fight among the other dogs and so tangle the traces.

At the mouth of the Talkeetna, one night after supper, Dub turned up a snowshoe rabbit. In a second the whole team was in full cry. A hundred yards away was a camp of the Northwest Police with fifty dogs, all huskies, who joined the chase. The rabbit sped down the river and off into a small creek. The rabbit ran lightly on the surface of the snow, while the dogs plowed through it. Buck led the pack, sixty strong, around bend after bend, but he could not gain on the rabbit. Buck's splendid body flashed forward, leap by leap, in the pale, white moonlight. And leap by leap, like some pale icy ghost, the snowshoe rabbit flashed on ahead.

From time to time, old instincts drive men out from cities and into the forests and the plains, where they kill things with pieces of lead shot from guns. This blood lust, this joy in killing, was shared by Buck, but in him it was far closer to the surface. He was running at the head of the pack, running the wild thing down, the living meat, to kill with his own teeth and feel the warm blood on his face.

There is a state of intense emotion that marks life's highest points. This state comes when one is most alive. Yet it also means a complete forgetfulness that one is alive. This emotion comes to an artist, caught up in a sheet of flame. It comes to a soldier on the battlefield, caught up in war. And it came to Buck, leading the pack, sounding the old wolf cry, straining after the food that was alive and that fled swiftly before him through the moonlight. He was overcome by the rush of life, the perfect joy of each muscle, joint, and sinew flying under the stars and over the surface of the snow.

But Spitz, cold and calculating as always, left the pack. He cut across a narrow neck of land where the creek made a long bend around. Buck did not know of this shortcut. As Buck rounded the bend with the icy ghost of a rabbit still flying before him, he saw another, larger figure leap into the rabbit's path. It was Spitz. The rabbit could not turn. As the white teeth broke its back in midair, it shrieked as loudly as a wounded man might shriek. At this sound, the full pack at Buck's heels raised a hell's chorus of delight.

Buck did not cry out. He did not stop running, but drove in on Spitz, shoulder to shoulder, so hard that he missed the throat. They rolled over and over in the powdery snow. Spitz got to his feet as quickly as if he had not been knocked down. He slashed Buck down the shoulder and jumped clear. Twice his teeth clipped together, like the steel jaws of a trap, as he backed away for better footing, with thin, snarling lips.

In a flash Buck knew it. The time had come. It was to the death. They circled about, snarling, ears laid back, keenly watchful for the advantage. The scene seemed familiar to Buck—the white woods, and earth, and moonlight, and the thrill of battle. Over the whiteness and silence brooded a ghostly calm. There was not the faintest whisper of air. Not a leaf quivered. Nothing moved, except the visible breaths of the dogs rising slowly in the frosty air.

These dogs, which really were poorly tamed wolves, had made short work of the snowshoe rabbit. Now they were drawn up in an expectant circle. They, too, were silent, their eyes gleaming and their breaths drifting slowly upward. To Buck it was nothing new or strange, this scene of old time. It was as though it had always been, as though it were the usual the way of things.

Spitz was an experienced fighter. From Spitzbergen through the Arctic, and across Canada and the Barrens, he had achieved victory over all manner of dogs. Although he felt bitter rage, he never let his rage blind him. In his passion to rip and destroy, he never forgot that his enemy felt the same passion. He never rushed until he was ready to receive a rush, and he never attacked until he had first defended an attack.

Buck strove without success to sink his teeth into the neck of the big white dog. Wherever his fangs tried to bite, they were met by the fangs of Spitz. Fang clashed against fang, and lips were cut and bleeding, but Buck could not break through his enemy's guard. Then he warmed up and surrounded Spitz in a whirlwind of rushes. Time and time again he tried for the snow-white throat, where life bubbled near the surface. Each time Spitz slashed him and got away. Then Buck took to rushing as though for the throat, but instead suddenly drawing back his head and curving in from the side. He would drive his shoulder at the shoulder of Spitz, like a ram, trying to overthrow him. But instead, Buck's shoulder was slashed each time, as Spitz leaped lightly away.

Spitz was untouched, while Buck was streaming with blood and panting hard. And all the while, the silent and wolf-like circle waited to finish off whichever dog went down. As Buck grew winded, Spitz took to rushing, and he kept Buck staggering for footing. Once Buck went over, and the whole circle of sixty dogs started up. But Buck recovered himself, almost in midair, and the circle sank down again and waited.

But Buck possessed a quality that made for greatness. He had imagination. He fought by instinct, but he could fight by head as well. He again rushed at Spitz, as though attempting the old shoulder trick. But at the last instant he swept low to the snow. His teeth closed on Spitz's left front leg. There was a crunch of breaking bone, and the white dog faced him on three legs. Buck tried three times to knock Spitz over. Then he repeated the trick and broke the dog's right front leg. Despite his pain and helplessness, Spitz struggled madly to keep up. He saw the silent circle, with gleaming eyes, lolling tongues, and silvery breaths drifting upward. The circle was closing in upon him, as he had seen similar circles close in on beaten opponents in the past. Only this time he was the one who was beaten.

There was no hope for him. Buck could not be stopped. Mercy could be found only in gentler climates. Buck maneuvered for the final rush. The circle had tightened till he could feel the breaths of the huskies on his sides. He could see them, beyond Spitz and to either side, half crouching for the spring. Their eyes were fixed on him. A pause seemed to fall. Every animal was motionless, as though turned to stone. Only Spitz quivered and bristled as he staggered back and forth, snarling with horrible menace,

as though to frighten off impending death. Then Buck sprang in and out. While he was in, shoulder at last squarely met shoulder. The dark circle became a dot on the moon-flooded snow as Spitz disappeared from view. Buck stood and looked on, the successful champion, the dominant beast who had made his kill and found it good.

Who Has Won to Mastership

"Eh? What I say? I speak true when I say dat Buck two devils."

So spoke François next morning when he discovered Spitz missing and Buck covered with wounds. He drew Buck to the fire and by the firelight pointed out Buck's wounds.

"Dat Spitz fight like hell," said Perrault, as he looked over the gaping rips and cuts.

"And dat Buck fight like two hells," answered François. "And now we make good time. No more Spitz, no more trouble, sure."

While Perrault packed the camp outfit and loaded the sled, François proceeded to harness the dogs. Buck trotted up to the place Spitz would have occupied as leader. But François did not notice him and brought Sol-leks to the prized position. In his judgment, Sol-leks was the best lead dog left. Buck sprang on Sol-leks in a fury, driving him back and standing in his place.

"Eh? Eh?" François cried, slapping his thighs and laughing. "Look at dat Buck. Him kill dat Spitz, him think to take de job."

"Go away, Chook!" he cried, but Buck refused to budge.

He took Buck by the scruff of the neck. Although Buck growled threateningly, François dragged him to one side and replaced Sol-leks. The old dog did not like it, and showed plainly that he was afraid of Buck. François was stubborn. But when he turned his back, Buck again removed Sol-leks, who was not at all unwilling to go.

François was angry. "Now, by Gar, I fix you!" he cried, coming back with a heavy club in his hand.

Buck remembered the man in the red sweater, and he backed up slowly. He did not attempt to charge in when Sol-leks was once more brought forward. But he circled just beyond the reach of the club, snarling with bitterness and rage. While he circled, he watched the club, so as to dodge it if thrown by François. He had become wise in the ways of clubs.

The driver went about his work. He called to Buck when he was ready to put him in his old place in front of Dave. Buck backed up two or three steps. François followed him, and Buck backed up again. After some time of this, François threw down the club, thinking that Buck feared a beating. But Buck was in open revolt. He did not want to escape a beating. He wanted leadership. It was his by right. He had earned it, and he would not be satisfied with anything less.

Perrault took a hand. Between them, they chased him around for most of an hour. They threw clubs at him. He dodged. They cursed him, and his fathers and mothers before him, and every generation that would come after him. They cursed every hair on his body and every drop of blood in his veins. He answered each curse with a snarl, and he kept out of their reach. He did not try to run away, but backed around and around the camp. He showed plainly that when he got what he wanted, he would come in and be good.

François sat down and scratched his head. Perrault looked at his watch and swore. Time was flying, and they should have been on the trail an hour earlier. François scratched his head again. He shook it and grinned in an embarrassed way at the courier. Perrault shrugged his shoulders as a sign that they were beaten. Then François went up to where Sol-leks stood and called to Buck. Buck laughed, in the way dogs laugh, but he kept his distance. François unhitched Sol-leks's traces and put him back in his old place. The team stood harnessed to the sled in an unbroken line, ready for the trail. The only place for Buck was at the front. Once more François called, and once more Buck laughed and stayed away.

"Throw down de club," Perrault commanded.

François obeyed. Buck then trotted in, laughing triumphantly, and swung around into position at the head of the team. His traces were fastened, the sled broken out, and with both men running they dashed out onto the river trail.

François had previously had a high opinion of Buck. But he found, while the day was still young, that his opinion had not been high enough. At a leap, Buck took up the duties of leadership. Where judgment was needed, and quick thinking and quick action, he was better even than Spitz—and Spitz was the best François had seen up to that time.

Buck was particularly good at giving the law and making the other dogs live up to it. Dave and Sol-leks did not mind the change in leadership. It was none of their business. Their business was to

work, and work mightily, in the traces. So long as they were not meddled with, they did not care what happened. For all they cared, the good-natured Billee could lead, so long as he kept order. The rest of the team, however, had grown unruly during Spitz's last days. Now, as Buck proceeded to lick them into shape, their surprise was great.

Pike, who pulled at Buck's heels, and who never put an ounce more of his weight against the breast-band than he had to, was quickly and often shaken for loafing. Before the first day was done, he was pulling more than ever in his life. The first day in camp, Joe, the sour one, was thoroughly punished, something that Spitz had never been able to do. With his superior weight, Buck simply smothered him and cut him up until he stopped snapping and began to whine for mercy.

The general tone of the team picked up immediately. It recovered its old-time togetherness. Once more the dogs leaped as one dog in the traces. At the Rink Rapids two native huskies, Teek and Koona, were added. The speed with which Buck broke them in took François's breath away.

"Never such a dog as dat Buck!" he cried. "No, never! Him worth one thousand dollar, by Gar! Eh? What you say, Perrault?"

And Perrault nodded. He was ahead of the record then, and gaining day by day. The trail was in excellent condition, well packed and hard. There was no new-fallen snow with which to contend, and it was not too cold. The temperature dropped to fifty below zero and stayed there the whole trip. The men took turns riding and running, and the dogs were kept on the jump, with few stops.

The Thirty Mile River had a better coating of ice than before, and they covered in one day going out what had taken them ten days going in. In one run they made a sixty-mile dash from the foot of Lake Labarge to the Whitehorse Rapids. Across Marsh, Tagish, and Bennett, seventy miles of lakes, they flew so fast that the man whose turn it was to run was pulled along behind the sled at the end of a rope. And on the last night of the second week, they topped White Pass and dropped down the sea slope, with the lights of Skagway at their feet.

It was a record run. Each day for fourteen days they had averaged forty miles. For three days Perrault and François paraded up and down the main street of Skagway and were showered with invitations to drink. The team was the constant center of a worshipful crowd of dog busters and drivers. Then three or four Western bad men tried to clean out the town, were shot full of holes for their efforts, and public interest turned to other subjects. Next came official orders. François called Buck to him, threw his arms around him, and wept over him. And that was the last of François and Perrault. Like other men, they passed out of Buck's life for good.

A Scot took charge of Buck and the other dogs. In company with a dozen other dog teams, they started back over the weary trail to Dawson. It was no light running now, nor record time. Instead it was heavy work each day, pulling a heavy load, for this was the mail train, carrying news from home to the men who sought gold under the shadow of the North Pole.

Buck did not like it. But he bore up well, taking pride in the work after the manner of Dave and Sol-leks. He saw to it that the other dogs did their fair share, whether they took pride in it or not. It was a dull life, operating in a steady way like a machine. One day was very like another. At a certain time each morning, the cooks turned out, fire was built, and breakfast was eaten. Then, while some broke camp, others harnessed the dogs. They were under way an hour or so before dawn. At night, camp was made. Some pitched the tents, others cut firewood and pine boughs for the beds, and still others carried water or ice for the cooks. Also, the dogs were fed. To them, this was the main event of the day. It was good, too, to loaf around, after the fish was eaten, for an hour or so with the other dogs, of whom there were more than a hundred. There were fierce fighters among them. But three battles with the fiercest brought Buck to mastery, so that when he bristled and showed his teeth, they got out of his way.

Best of all, perhaps, he liked to lie near the fire, hind legs crouched under him, front legs stretched out, head raised, and eyes blinking dreamily at the flames. Sometimes he thought of Judge Miller's big house in the sun-kissed Santa Clara Valley, and of the cement swimming tank, and Ysabel, the Mexican hairless, and Toots, the Japanese pug. But oftener he remembered the man in the red sweater, the death of Curly, the great fight with Spitz, and the good things he had eaten or would like to eat. He was not homesick. The Sunland was very dim and distant, and such memories had no power over him. Far more powerful were the memories inherited from his ancestors, which made things seem familiar even though he had never seen them before. Buck's instincts were nothing more than these memories of his ancestors turned into habit. They had fallen out of use, but now, in him, quickened and became alive again.

Sometimes as he crouched there, blinking dreamily at the flames, it seemed that he was at another, different fire. It seemed, as he crouched by this other fire, that he saw another and different man from the cook before him. This other man had shorter legs and longer arms, with muscles that were stringy and knotty rather than round and swelling. The hair of this man was long and matted, and under the hair his head slanted back from the eyes. He spoke strange sounds, and he seemed very much afraid of the darkness, into which he peered continually. In his hand, which hung halfway between his knee and his foot, he clutched a stick with a heavy stone attached at one end. He was almost naked, clothed only in a ragged and burned skin that hung partway down his back. There was much hair on his body. In some places, across his chest and shoulders and down the outside of his arms and thighs, the hair was matted almost into a thick fur. He did not stand upright, but instead leaned forward from the hips, his legs bent at the knees. There was a peculiar spring to his body, almost like a cat. He was constantly alert, as if he lived in never-ending fear of things both seen and unseen.

At other times this hairy man squatted by the fire with his head between his knees and slept. His elbows were on his knees, and his hands were clasped above his head, as if to keep off the rain with the hairy arms. And beyond that fire, in the darkness all around, Buck could see many gleaming coals, two by two, always two by two. He knew that these were the eyes of great beasts of prey. And he could hear the crashing of their bodies through the undergrowth, and the noises they made at night. And dreaming there by the Yukon bank, with lazy eyes blinking at the fire, these sounds and sights of another world would make the hair rise along his back, and stand on end across his shoulders and up his neck. Then he would whimper low, or growl softly, until the cook shouted at him, "Hey, you, Buck, wake up!" At that, the other world would vanish, and the real world would come back into his eyes. And he would get up and yawn and stretch, as if he had been asleep.

With the sled loaded down with mail, it was a hard trip. The heavy work wore them down. They were below normal weight and in poor condition when they reached Dawson. They should have had a ten days' rest, or a week at least. But in only two days' time, they dropped down the Yukon bank from the Barracks, loaded with letters for the outside. The dogs were tired and the drivers grumbling. To make matters worse, it snowed every day. This meant a soft trail, greater friction on the runners, and heavier pulling for the dogs. Yet the drivers were fair through it all, and they did their best for the animals.

Each night the dogs were attended to first. They ate before the drivers ate, and no man went to sleep until he had seen to the feet of the dogs he drove. Still, their strength went down. Since the beginning of the winter, they had traveled eighteen hundred miles, dragging sleds the whole weary distance. Eighteen hundred miles will begin to wear down even the toughest. Buck stood it, keeping the other dogs up to their work. But he, too, was very tired. Billee cried and whimpered regularly in his sleep each night. Joe was sourer than ever, and Sol-leks could not be approached at all, blind side or other side.

But it was Dave who suffered most of all. Something had gone wrong with him. He became more gloomy and crabby. When camp was pitched, he made his nest immediately, where his driver fed him. Once out of the harness and lying down, he did not get up again until harnessing time in the morning. Sometimes, when he was jerked by a sudden stop of the sled, or when he was straining to start, he would cry out in pain. The driver examined him, but could find nothing. All the drivers became interested in his case. They talked it over at mealtime and over their last pipes before going to bed, and one night they held a meeting. Dave was brought from his nest to the fire, and was pressed and prodded until he cried out many times. Something was wrong inside, but they could locate no broken bones. They could not figure it out.

By the time Cassiar Bar was reached, Dave was so weak that he was falling over and over again in the traces. The Scot called a halt and took him out of the team. He put the next dog, Sol-leks, in Dave's place by the sled. The driver intended to rest Dave, letting him run free behind the sled. Sick as he was, Dave did not want to be taken out. He grunted and growled as the traces were unfastened, and he whimpered brokenheartedly when he saw Sol-leks in the place where he had served so long. For he had the pride of a sled dog, and even though sick unto death, he could not bear that another dog should do his work.

When the sled started, Dave struggled in the soft snow alongside the beaten trail. He repeatedly attacked Sol-leks, rushing against him and trying to push him off into the soft snow on the other side, trying to jump inside the traces and get between him and the sled, and all the while whining and yelping and crying with grief and pain. The Scot tried to drive him away with the whip. But he paid no attention to the sting of the whip, and the man did not have the heart to strike harder. Dave refused to run quietly on the trail behind the sled, where the going was easy. He continued to struggle alongside in the soft snow, where the going was most difficult, until he was exhausted. Then he fell, and lay where he fell, howling mournfully as the long train of sleds passed by.

With the last trace of his strength, he managed to stagger along behind until the train made another stop. Then he struggled past the other sleds to his own, where he stood beside Sol-leks. His driver delayed a moment to get a light for his pipe from the man behind. Then he returned and started his dogs. They swung out on the trail with remarkable ease, turned their heads nervously, and stopped in surprise. The driver was surprised, too, for the sled had not moved. He called to the other drivers to see the sight. Dave had bitten through both of Sol-leks's traces and was standing directly in front of the sled in his proper place.

He begged with his eyes to remain there. The driver did not know what to do. The other drivers talked of how a dog could break its heart by having its work taken from it, even though the work was killing it. They remembered dogs they had known who, too old for the work, or injured, had died because they were cut out of the traces. Also they thought it would be an act of mercy, since Dave was going to die anyway, to let him die in the traces, easy at heart and contented. So Dave was harnessed in again, and proudly he pulled as of old, though more than once he cried out from the bite of his inward hurt. Several times he fell down and was dragged in the traces, and once the sled ran up on him, so that he limped in one of his hind legs.

But he held out until camp was reached, when his driver made a place for him by the fire. The next morning he was too weak to travel. At harness-up time, he tried to crawl to his driver. With a huge effort, he got on his feet, staggered, and fell. Then he inched his way slowly forward toward where the harnesses were being put on the other dogs. He would move his front legs forward, then drag up his body with a sort of hitching movement, then advance his front legs and hitch ahead again for a few more inches. Finally his strength left him. The last the other dogs saw of him, he lay gasping in the snow and yearning toward them. But they could hear him mournfully howling until they passed out of sight behind a belt of river timber.

Here the train was halted. The Scot slowly went back to the camp they had left. The men stopped talking. A revolver shot rang out. The man hurried back. The whips snapped, the bells tinkled merrily, the sleds churned along the trail. But Buck knew, and every dog knew, what had taken place behind the belt of river trees.

5 *The Toil of Trace and Trail*

Thirty days from the time it left Dawson, the Salt Water Mail, with Buck and his team at the front, arrived in Skagway. They were in a sad state, worn out and worn down. Buck's 140 pounds had shrunk to 115 pounds. The rest of the dogs had lost even more, although they were lighter than Buck to begin with. Pike, the dog who often pretended to be injured, now had a genuine limp. Sol-leks, too, was limping, and Dub was suffering from a pulled shoulder blade.

They were all terribly footsore. No spring or rebound was left in them. Their feet fell heavily on the trail, jolting their bodies and adding to the fatigue of a day's travel. There was nothing the matter with them except that they were dead tired. It was not the tiredness that comes from brief and intense effort, from which one recovers in a few hours. It was the dead-tiredness that comes from the slow and lengthy draining of strength through months of heavy work. There was no power of recovery left, no reserve strength to call upon. It had been all used, the last least bit of it. Every muscle, every fiber, every cell was tired, dead tired. And there was reason for it. In less than five months they had traveled twenty-five hundred miles, during the last eighteen hundred of which they had had only five days' rest. When they arrived at Skagway, they were on their last legs. They could barely keep the traces taut, and on downgrades they just managed to keep out of the way of the sled.

"Mush on, poor sore feets," the driver encouraged them as they trotted unsteadily down the main street of Skagway. "Dis is de last. Den we get one long rest. Eh? For sure. One bully long rest."

The drivers confidently expected a long stopover. They themselves had just covered twelve hundred miles with two days' rest, and both fairness and common sense said that they deserved to loaf for a while. But so many men had rushed to the Klondike, and so many sweethearts, wives, and relatives had not rushed in, that mountains of mail were piling up. In addition, there were official orders to be delivered. Fresh teams of Hudson Bay dogs were to take the places of those worthless for the trail. The worthless ones were to be got rid of, and, since dogs count for little against dollars, they were to be sold.

Three days passed, by which time Buck and the other dogs learned how really tired and weak they were. Then, on the morning of the fourth day, two men from the States came along and bought them, harness and all, for a song. The men called each other Hal and Charles. Charles was a middle-aged, pale man, with weak and watery eyes. He had a mustache that twisted fiercely and vigorously up, hiding the limp, drooping lip beneath it. Hal was a youngster of nineteen or twenty, with a big Colt's revolver and a hunting knife strapped about him on a belt that fairly bristled with cartridges. This belt was the most obvious thing about him. It advertised his lack of maturity, a lack that was complete and absolute. Both men obviously were out of place, and why people like them should adventure to the North is one of those mysteries that cannot be understood.

Buck heard the bargaining, saw the money pass between the man and the Government agent, and knew that the Scot and the mail-train drivers were passing out of his life, like Perrault and François and the others who had gone before. When he was driven with the other dogs to the new owners' camp, Buck found a scruffy, untidy arrangement. The tent was half-stretched, the dishes were unwashed, and everything was in disorder. Also, he saw a woman. The men called her Mercedes. She was Charles's wife and Hal's sister—a nice family party.

Buck watched them, worried, as they proceeded to take down the tent and load the sled. There was a great deal of effort in the way they did things, but no businesslike method. The tent was rolled into an awkward bundle three times larger than it should have been. The tin dishes were packed away unwashed. Mercedes continually got in the way of her men, and she kept up an unbroken stream of advice and criticism. When they put a clothes sack on the front of the sled, she suggested it should go on the back. When they put it on the back, and covered it over with a couple of other bundles, she found overlooked items that could go nowhere but in that one sack, and they unloaded again.

Three men from a neighboring tent came over and watched, grinning and winking at each other.

"You've got a right smart load as it is," said one of them, "and it's not me should tell you your business, but I wouldn't tote that tent along if I was you."

"Undreamed of!" cried Mercedes, throwing up

her hands in dainty dismay. "However in the world could I manage without a tent?"

"It's springtime, and you won't get any more cold weather," the man replied.

She shook her head decisively, and Charles and Hal put the last odds and ends on top of the mountainous load.

"Think it will ride?" one of the men asked.

"Why shouldn't it?" Charles demanded rather shortly.

"Oh, that's all right, that's all right," the man said meekly. "I was just a-wondering, that is all. It seemed a mite top heavy."

Charles turned his back and drew the lashings down as well as he could, which was not at all well.

"And of course the dogs can hike along all day with that contraption behind them," declared another man.

"Certainly," said Hal, with freezing politeness. He took hold of the gee pole with one hand and swung his whip with the other. "Mush!" he shouted. "Mush on there!"

The dogs sprang against the breastbands, strained hard for a few moments, then relaxed. They were unable to move the sled.

"The lazy brutes, I'll show them," he cried, getting ready to lash out at them with the whip.

But Mercedes interfered, crying out, "Oh, Hal, you mustn't." She caught hold of the whip and tore it from him. "The poor dears! Now you must promise you won't be harsh with them for the rest of the trip, or I won't go a step."

"Precious lot you know about dogs," her brother sneered, "and I wish you would leave me alone.

They're lazy, I tell you, and you've got to whip them to get anything out of them. That's their way. You ask anyone. Ask one of those men."

Mercedes looked at them in distress. Horror at the sight of pain was written in her pretty face.

"They're weak as water, if you want to know," came the reply from one of the men. "Plumb tuckered out, that's what's the matter. They need a rest."

"Rest be ——," said Hal, with his beardless lips. Mercedes said, "Oh!" in pain and sorrow at the oath.

But she was loyal to her family, and she rushed at once to the defence of her brother. "Never mind that man," she said sharply. "You're driving our dogs, and you do what you think best with them."

Again Hal's whip fell on the dogs. They threw themselves against the breastbands, dug their feet into the snow, and put forth all their strength. The sled held as though it were an anchor. After two efforts, they stood still, panting. The whip was whistling savagely, when once more Mercedes stepped in. She dropped on her knees before Buck, with tears in her eyes, and put her arms around his neck.

"You poor, poor dears!" she cried sympathetically. "Why don't you pull hard? Then you wouldn't be whipped." Buck did not like her, but he was feeling too miserable to resist. He took it as part of the day's miserable work.

One of the onlookers, who had been clenching his teeth to hold back his anger, now spoke up:

"It's not that I care a whoop what becomes of you, but for the dogs' sakes I just want to tell you, you can help them a mighty lot by breaking out that sled. The runners are froze fast. Throw your weight against the gee pole, right and left, and break it out."

They tried a third time. This time, following the advice, Hal broke out the runners, which had indeed been frozen to the snow. The overloaded and awkward sled moved ahead, Buck and the other dogs struggling frantically under the rain of blows. A hundred yards ahead, the path turned and sloped steeply into the main street. It would have taken an experienced man to keep the top-heavy sled right side up, and Hal was not such a man. As they swung into the turn, the sled went over, spilling half its load through the loose lashings. The dogs never stopped. The lightened sled bounced on its side behind them. They were angry because of the ill treatment they had received and the unjust load. Buck was furious. He broke into a run, the team following his lead. Hal cried, "Whoa! whoa!" but they paid no attention. Hal tripped and was pulled off his feet. The overturned sled ground over him, and the dogs dashed ahead, adding to the amusement of Skagway as they scattered the rest of the outfit along its main street.

Thoughtful citizens caught the dogs and gathered up the scattered belongings. Also, they gave advice. Half the load and twice the dogs, if they ever expected to reach Dawson, they said. Hal and his sister and brother-in-law listened unwillingly. Then they pitched their tent and began to overhaul their outfit. Men laughed at the canned goods that were turned out, for canned goods on the Long Trail are a thing to dream about. "Blankets for a hotel," said one of the men who laughed and helped. "Half as many is still too much. Get rid of them. Throw away that tent, and all those dishes. Who is going to wash them, anyway? Good Lord, do you think you're traveling on a Pullman?

And so it went, the unavoidable getting rid of what was not needed. Mercedes cried when her clothes bags were dumped on the ground and article after article was thrown out. She cried in general, and she cried in particular over each thing that was discarded. She clasped her hands around her knees, rocking back and forth as if her heart were broken. She said she would not go an inch, not for a dozen Charleses. She appealed to everybody and to everything. Finally she wiped her eyes and proceeded to throw away even those things that she could not do without. And in her enthusiasm, she attacked the belongings of her men after she had finished with her own, and went through them like a tornado.

When they were done, the outfit, although cut in half, was still an impressive bulk. Charles and Hal went out in the evening and bought six Outside dogs. These, added to the six of the original team, and Teek and Koona, the huskies obtained at the Rink Rapids on the previous trip, brought the team up to fourteen. But the Outside dogs did not amount to much. Three were short-haired pointers, one was a Newfoundland, and the other two were mongrels of uncertain breed. They did not seem to know anything, these newcomers. Buck and his comrades looked on them with disgust. Although Buck quickly taught them their places and what not to do, he could not teach them what to do. They did not take kindly to trace and trail. Except for the two mongrels, they were confused and spirit-broken by the strange, savage environment in which they found themselves and by the bad treatment they had received. The two mongrels had no spirit at all. The only things breakable about them were their bones.

With the newcomers hopeless and miserable, and the old team worn out by twenty-five hundred miles of continuous trail, the outlook was anything but bright. The two men, however, were quite cheerful. And they were proud, too. They were doing the thing in style, with fourteen dogs. They had seen other sleds depart over the Pass for Dawson, or come in from Dawson, but they had never seen a sled with as many as fourteen dogs. In the nature of Arctic travel, there was a reason why fourteen dogs should not drag one sled. The reason was simply that one sled could not carry enough food for fourteen dogs. But Charles and Hal did not know this. They had worked the trip out with a pencil, so much to a dog, so many dogs, so many days. Mercedes looked over their shoulders and nodded. It was all so very simple.

Late next morning Buck led the long team up the street. There was nothing lively about it, no snap or go in him and his fellows. They were starting dead weary. Four times he had covered the distance between Salt Water and Dawson. The knowledge that he was facing the same trail once more made him bitter. His heart was not in the work, nor was the heart of any of the dogs. The Outsides were timid and frightened. The Insides had no confidence in their masters.

Buck felt vaguely that one could not depend on these two men and the women. They did not know how to do anything. As the days went by, it became obvious that they could not learn. They were careless in all things, without order or discipline. It took them half the night to pitch a messy camp, and half the morning to break that camp and get the sled loaded.

They loaded it so carelessly that they spent much of the day stopping and rearranging the load. Some days they did not make ten miles. On other days they were unable to get started at all. And on no day did they make more than half the distance that was the basis of their dog-food computation.

They could not avoid running short of dog food. But they hastened it by overfeeding, bringing closer the day when underfeeding would begin. The Outside dogs, whose digestions had not been trained to make the most of little, had huge appetites. And when, in addition to this, the worn-out huskies pulled weakly, Hal decided that the usual ration was too small. He doubled it. And to cap it all, when Mercedes, with tears in her pretty eyes and a shake in her voice, could not coax him to give the dogs still more, she stole from the fish sacks and fed them on the sly. But it was not food that Buck and the huskies needed. They needed rest. And though they were making poor time, the heavy load that they dragged drained their strength.

Then came the underfeeding. Hal awoke one day to the fact that his dog food was half gone, while they had covered only a quarter of the distance they had to go. He also realized that, for love or money, no additional dog food could be obtained. So he cut down to less than the usual ration, and at the same time he tried to increase the day's travel. His sister and brother-in-law backed him up. But they were held back by their heavy outfit and their own lack of skill. It was a simple matter to give the dogs less food. But it was impossible to make the dogs travel faster, and they were kept from traveling longer hours by their own inability to get under way earlier in the morning. Not only did they not know how to work dogs, but they did not know how to work themselves.

The first to go was Dub. Poor blundering thief that he was, always getting caught and punished, he had nonetheless been a faithful worker. But without either treatment or rest, his wrenched shoulder blade went from bad to worse. Finally Hal shot him with the big Colt's revolver. It is a saying of the country that an Outside dog starves to death on the ration of a husky, so on half a husky's ration, the six Outside dogs could do nothing less than die. The Newfoundland went first, followed by the three short-haired pointers. The two mongrels hung more stubbornly onto life, but they, too, went in the end.

By this time, all the pleasant and gentle customs of the Southland had fallen away from the three people. With its glamour and romance gone, Arctic travel became too harsh a reality for them to deal with. Mercedes stopped weeping over the dogs, since she was too occupied now with weeping over herself and with quarreling with her husband and brother. Quarreling was the one thing they were never too tired to do. Their bad temper arose out of their misery. It increased as the misery increased, doubled it, and finally left it far behind. The wonderful patience of the trail comes to men who work hard and suffer much, and they remain sweet of speech and kindly. But it did not come to these two men and the woman. They had no notion of such patience. They were stiff and in pain. Their muscles ached, their bones ached, their very hearts ached. Because of this, they became sharp of speech, and hard words were the first thing they said in the morning and the last at night.

Charles and Hal argued whenever Mercedes gave them a chance. Each of them believed that he did more than his share of the work, and neither held back from speaking this belief at every opportunity. Sometimes Mercedes sided with her husband, sometimes with her brother. The result was a beautiful and unending family quarrel. Starting from a dispute as to who should chop a few sticks for the fire (a dispute that concerned only Charles and Hal), the rest of the family soon would be dragged in, including fathers, mothers, uncles, cousins, people thousands of miles away, and some of them dead. It is hard to believe that Hal's views on art, or on the sort of society plays his uncle wrote, had anything to do with the chopping of a few sticks of firewood. Nevertheless, the quarrel was as likely to be about that as about Charles's political prejudices. And only Mercedes knew what Charles's sister's gossiping had to do with the building of a Yukon fire. She supplied many opinions on that subject, and incidentally on a few other unpleasant traits to be found in her husband's family. Meanwhile the fire remained unbuilt, the camp half pitched, and the dogs unfed.

Mercedes nursed a special complaint. She was pretty and soft, and she had been courteously treated all her life. But the present treatment by her husband and brother was everything but courteous. She was used to being helpless. They complained. They had rejected what she saw as her most basic right as a woman, so she made their lives unbearable. She no longer considered the dogs, and because she was sore and tired, she insisted on riding on the sled. She was pretty and soft, but she weighed 120 pounds—a last straw to the load dragged by the weak and starving animals. She rode for days, until the dogs fell in the traces and the sled stood still. Charles and Hal begged her to get off and walk, pleaded with her, begged with her. Meanwhile she wept and told Heaven the story of their brutality.

On one occasion they took her off the sled by force. They never did it again. She let her legs go limp like a spoiled child, and sat down on the trail. They went on their way, but she did not move. After they had traveled three miles, they unloaded the sled, came back for her, and put her on the sled again.

Because of their own misery, they had no pity for the suffering of the animals. Hal's idea, which he practiced on others, was that one must get hardened. He had started out preaching it to his sister and his brother-in-law. After having no success with them, he hammered it into the dogs with a club. At the Five Fingers the dog food gave out. A toothless old squaw offered to trade them a few pounds of frozen horse hide for the Colt's revolver that kept the big hunting knife company on Hal's hip. This hide was a poor substitute for food. It had been stripped from the starved horses of the cattlemen six months earlier. In its frozen state it was more like strips of iron than like food. When a dog wrestled it into its stomach, the hide thawed into thin, leathery strings and a mass of short hair. It irritated the dogs' stomachs, could not be digested, and was completely lacking in nutrition.

And through it all, Buck staggered along at the head of the team as if he were in a nightmare. He pulled when he could. When he could no longer pull, he fell down and stayed there until blows from a whip or a club drove him to his feet again. All the stiffness and gloss had gone out of his beautiful furry coat. The hair hung down, limp and scruffy, or matted with dried blood where Hal's club had bruised him. His muscles had wasted away to knotty strings, and the flesh pads had disappeared. Each rib and every other bone in his frame was clearly outlined through the loose, wrinkled skin. It was heartbreaking. Only Buck's heart was unbreakable. The man in the red sweater had proved that.

As it was with Buck, so it was with the other dogs. They were walking skeletons. There were seven altogether, including him. In their very great misery, they no longer felt the bite of the lash or the bruise of the club. The pain of beating was dull and distant, just as the things their eyes saw and their ears heard seemed dull and distant. They were not half alive, or even a quarter alive. They were simply seven bags of bones in which sparks of life fluttered faintly. When a halt was made, they dropped down in the traces like dead dogs. The spark dimmed and paled and seemed to go out. And when the club or whip fell upon them, the spark fluttered up feebly, and they stumbled to their feet and staggered on.

There came a day when Billee, the good-natured, fell and could not rise. Hal had traded off his revolver, so he took the axe and knocked Billee on the head as he lay in the traces. Then he cut the carcass out of the harness and dragged it to one side. Buck saw, and the other dogs saw, and they knew that this thing was very close to them. On the next day, Koona went. Now only five remained. Joe was too far gone to be harmful. Pike, crippled and limping, was only half conscious, and not conscious

enough to loaf. Sol-leks, the one-eyed, was still faithful to the work of trace and trail, and sad because he had so little strength with which to pull. Teek, who had not traveled so far that winter, now was beaten more than the others, because he was fresher. And Buck, still at the head of the team, no longer enforced discipline. Blind with weakness half the time, he kept the trail by the dim look of it and the dim feel of his feet.

It was beautiful spring weather, but neither dogs nor humans were aware of it. Each day the sun rose earlier and set later. Dawn came at three in the morning, and twilight lingered until nine at night. The whole long day was a blaze of sunshine. The ghostly winter silence had given way to the great spring murmur of awakening life. This murmur arose from all the land, filled with the joy of living. It came from the things that lived and moved again, things that had been as good as dead during the long months of frost. The sap was rising in the pines. The willows and aspens were bursting out in young buds. Shrubs and vines were putting on fresh dress of green. Crickets sang in the night. In the days, all sorts of creeping, crawling things rustled forth into the sun. Partridges and woodpeckers were booming and knocking in the forest. Squirrels were chattering, birds singing, and overhead honked the wild geese flying up from the south in wedges that split the air.

From every hill slope came the trickle of running water, the music of unseen fountains. All things were thawing, bending, snapping. The Yukon was straining to break loose from the ice that held it down. It ate the ice away from beneath, while the sun ate it from above. Air holes formed, and cracks appeared and spread apart. Whole thin sections of ice fell through into the river. And amid all this awakening life, the two men, the woman, and the huskies staggered like travelers to death.

With the dogs falling, Mercedes weeping and riding, Hal swearing harmlessly, and Charles's eyes watering vaguely, they staggered into John Thornton's camp at the mouth of the White River. When they halted, the dogs dropped down as though they had all been struck dead. Mercedes dried her eyes and looked at John Thornton. Charles sat down on a log to rest. He sat very slowly and carefully because of his great stiffness. Hal did the talking. John Thornton was whittling the last touches on an axe handle he had made from a stick of birch. He whittled, and listened, and gave brief replies. When it was asked, he gave advice. He knew these kinds of people, and when he gave them his advice he was sure that it would not be followed.

"They told us up above that the bottom was dropping out of the trail, and that the best thing for us to do was lay over," Hal said. This was his answer to Thornton's warning against taking any more chances on the rotten ice. "They told us we couldn't make White River, and here we are." This last with a sneering ring of triumph in it.

"They told you the truth," John Thornton answered. "The bottom is likely to drop out at any moment. Only fools, with the blind luck of fools, could have made it. I tell you straight, I wouldn't risk my carcass on that ice for all the gold in Alaska."

"That's because you're not a fool, I suppose," said Hal. "All the same, we'll get on to Dawson." He uncoiled his whip. "Get up there, Buck! Hi! Get up there! Mush on!"

Thornton went on whittling. He knew there was no point in trying to keep a fool from being foolish. And two or three fools, more or less, would not make much difference in the world.

But the team did not get up at the command. It had been a long time now that only blows could get it on its feet. The whip flashed out. John Thornton compressed his lips. Sol-leks was the first to crawl to his feet. Teek followed. Joe came next, yelping with pain. Pike made painful efforts. Twice he fell over from halfway up. On the third try, he managed to rise. Buck made no effort. He lay quietly where he had fallen. The lash bit into him again and again, but he neither whined nor struggled. Several times Thornton started to speak, but changed his mind. Tears came into his eyes. As the whipping continued, he arose and walked up and down, as if not sure what he should do.

This was the first time Buck had failed. That alone was enough to drive Hal into a rage. He traded his whip for the usual club. Buck refused to move under the rain of heavier blows that now fell on him. Like the other dogs, he was barely able to get up. But unlike them, he had made up his mind that he would not get up. He had a vague feeling of approaching doom. He had felt this feeling strongly when they pulled into this place, and it had not left him. What with the thin and rotten ice he had felt under his feet all day, he sensed disaster close at hand. It was out there ahead on the ice, where his master was trying to drive him. He refused to move. He had suffered so greatly and was so far gone, that the blows did not hurt much. And as the blows continued to fall on him, the spark of life within him flickered and went down. It was nearly out. He felt strangely numb. As though from a great distance, he was aware that he was being beaten. The last sensations of pain left him. He no longer felt anything, though very faintly he could hear the club hitting his body. But it was no longer his body, it seemed so far away.

John Thornton stood over Buck, struggling to control himself. He was shaking so with rage that he could not speak.

"If you strike that dog again, I will kill you," he managed at last to say in a choking voice.

"It's my dog," Hal replied, wiping the blood from his mouth as he came back. "Get out of my way, or I'll fix you. I'm going to Dawson."

Thornton stood between him and Buck. He showed no intention of getting out of the way. Hal drew his long hunting knife. Mercedes screamed, cried, and laughed uncontrollably. Thornton rapped Hal's knuckles with the axe handle, knocking the knife to the ground. He rapped Hal's knuckles again as he tried to pick it up. Then he stooped, picked it up himself, and with two strokes cut Buck's traces.

Hal had no fight left in him. Besides, his hands were full with his sister—or rather, his arms were full. Buck was now too near dead to be of further use in hauling the sled. A few minutes later they pulled out from the bank and down the river. Buck heard them go and raised his head to see. Pike was leading, Sol-leks was in front of the sled, and between were Joe and Teek. They were limping and staggering. Mercedes was riding the loaded sled. Hal guided at the gee pole, and Charles stumbled along in the rear.

As Buck watched them, Thornton knelt beside him and with rough, kindly hands searched for broken bones. His search found nothing more than many bruises and a state of terrible starvation. By the time he was finished, the sled was a quarter of a mile away. Dog and man watched it crawling over the ice. Suddenly, they saw its back end drop down, as if it had fallen into a rut. The gee pole, with Hal clinging to it, jerked into the air. They could hear Mercedes screaming. Charles turned and took one step to run back. Then a whole section of ice gave way, and dogs and humans disappeared. A yawning hole was all that was to be seen. The bottom had dropped out of the trail.

John Thornton and Buck looked at each other.

"You poor devil," said John Thornton, and Buck licked his hand.

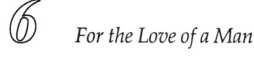

6 *For the Love of a Man*

The previous December, when John Thornton froze his feet, his partners made him comfortable and left him to get well. They themselves went up the river to get out a raft of logs for Dawson. At the time he rescued Buck, Thornton was still limping slightly. But with the continued warm weather, even the slight limp left him. And here, lying by the river bank through the long spring days, watching the running water, listening lazily to the songs of the birds and the hum of nature, Buck slowly won back his strength.

After one has traveled three thousand miles, a rest is very welcome. As his wounds healed, and his muscles swelled, and the flesh came back to cover his bones, Buck grew lazy. For that matter, they were all loafing—Buck, and John Thornton, and Skeet, and Night. They were waiting for the raft that would carry them down to Dawson. Skeet was a little Irish setter who early made friends with Buck. In his dying condition, Buck had not been able to resist her first advances. She had the doctor trait, which some dogs have. As a mother cat washes her kittens, so she washed and cleaned Buck's wounds. Regularly, each morning after he had finished his breakfast, she carried out her self-appointed task, until he came to look for her care as much as he did for Thornton's.

Night, equally friendly, was a huge black dog, half bloodhound and half deerhound, with eyes that laughed and constant good nature.

To Buck's surprise, these dogs showed no feelings of jealousy toward him. They seemed to share the kindliness and good will of John Thornton. As Buck grew stronger, they lured him into all sorts of ridiculous games, which Thornton himself could not keep from joining. In this fashion, Buck romped through his getting well and into a new existence. For the first time he felt love, genuine, passionate love. This he had never experienced at Judge Miller's down in the sun-kissed Santa Clara Valley. With the Judge's sons, hunting and tramping, it had been a working partnership. With the Judge's grandsons, it was a sort of stuffy guardianship. With the Judge himself, it had been a stately and dignified friendship. But love that was feverish and burning, that was worship, that was madness, it had taken John Thornton to awaken.

This man had saved his life, which was something. But in addition, he was the ideal master. Other men saw to their dogs from a sense of duty and good business. Thornton took care of his dogs as if they were his children, because he could not help it. And he saw further. He never forgot a kindly greeting or a cheering word, and to sit down for a long talk with the dogs (gas, he called it) was as pleasant for him as for them. He had a way of taking Buck's head roughly between his hands, and resting his own head on Buck's, and shaking him back and forth. All the time he would call Buck bad names that to Buck were love names. Buck knew no greater joy than that rough embrace and the sound of mur-

mured oaths. At each jerk back and forth it seemed as if his heart would be shaken out of his body, so great was his joy. And when he was released and sprang to his feet, his mouth laughing, his eyes eloquent, his body motionless, John Thornton would admiringly exclaim, "God! You can all but speak!"

Buck had a way of expressing his love that was almost hurtful. He would seize Thornton's hand in his mouth and close so fiercely that the flesh showed teeth marks for some time afterward. And as Buck understood the oaths to be love words, so the man understood the pretended bite to be a caress.

For the most part, however, Buck expressed his love from a distance. Although he went wild with happiness when Thornton touched him or spoke to him, he did not seek these signs of Thornton's love. Skeet would shove her nose under Thornton's hand and nudge and nudge until he petted her. Night would rest his great head on Thornton's knee. Unlike them, Buck was content to adore Thornton from farther away. He would lie by the hour at Thornton's feet, eager and alert. He looked up at Thornton's face, studied it, followed each change of expression with the sharpest interest. Or he would lie farther away, to the rear or side, watching the outline of the man and the movements of his body. And often, so strong was the friendship between them, the strength of Buck's gaze would cause John Thornton to turn his head around. Without speaking, he would return the gaze, his heart shining out of his eyes in the same way that Buck's heart shone out.

For a long time after his rescue, Buck did not like Thornton to get out of his sight. From the moment Thornton left the tent until he entered it again, Buck would follow at his heels. After the series of temporary masters that he had had since he came into the Northland, Buck was afraid that no master could be permanent. He was afraid that Thornton would go out of his life as Perrault and François and the Scot had gone out of it. Even at night, in his dreams, this fear haunted him. Then he would wake up and creep through the cold to the flap of the tent, where he would stand and listen to the sound of his master's breathing.

Buck's great love for John Thornton suggested a soft, civilizing influence in his life. But the strain of the primitive, which the Northland had awakened in him, was still alive and active. He was faithful and devoted, but he kept his wildness and cleverness. He was a thing of the wild, who had come in from the wild to sit by John Thornton's fire. He was no longer a dog of the soft Southland, stamped with the marks of civilization. Because of his very great love, he could not steal from Thornton. But from any other man, in any other camp, he did not hesitate an instant, and he stole with such cunning that he was never caught.

His face and body were scarred by the teeth of many dogs. He fought as fiercely as ever, and more shrewdly. He did not fight Skeet and Night. They were too good-natured to quarrel with, and besides, they belonged to John Thornton. But any strange dog, regardless of his bravery, soon admitted Buck's mastery. Otherwise he found himself fighting for his life against a terrible opponent. And Buck was merciless. He had learned well the law of club and fang, and he never gave up an advantage or held back from a rival he had started on the way to Death. He had learned from Spitz, and from the chief fighting dogs of the police and mail, that there was no middle way. He must defeat or be defeated. It was a weakness to show mercy, which did not exist in the primitive life. Mercy was misunderstood for fear, and that kind of misunderstanding led to death. Kill or be killed, eat or be eaten. That was the law, passed down from the beginning of Time, and he obeyed it.

He was older than the days he had seen and the breaths he had drawn. He linked the past with the present, and the eternity behind him throbbed through him in a mighty rhythm. He sat by John Thornton's fire, a broad-chested dog, white-fanged and long-furred. But behind him were the ghosts of all sorts of dogs, half wolves, and wild wolves. They tasted the meat he ate and thirsted for the water he drank. They scented the wind with him. They listened with him, and told him the sounds made by the wild life in the forest. They directed his mood and his actions. They lay down to sleep with him, and they dreamed with him and beyond him. They became what he dreamed about.

These ghosts called so powerfully to Buck that each day mankind and its ways slipped farther away from him. A call was sounding deep in the forest, mysterious and thrilling. Whenever Buck heard this call, he felt driven to turn his back on the fire and on the beaten earth around it, and to plunge into the forest, and on and on. He did not know where he was going, or why. But when he found himself at the soft, unbroken earth and the green shade of the deepest forest, the love for John Thornton drew him back to the fire again.

Thornton alone held him. The rest of mankind

did not matter. Travelers would praise or pet him, but he was cold under it all, and sometimes would get up and walk away. When Thornton's partners, Hans and Pete, arrived on the long-awaited raft, Buck refused to notice them until he learned they were Thornton's friends. After that, he put up with them quietly, accepting favors from them as if he were the one doing the favor. They were the same kind of person as Thornton, living close to the earth, thinking simply, and seeing clearly. By the time they swung the raft into the big eddy by the sawmill at Dawson, they understood Buck and his ways. They did not insist on closeness such as they felt with Skeet and Night.

Buck's love for Thornton, however, seemed to grow and grow. He was the only man who could put a pack on Buck's back when they traveled in the summer. When Thornton commanded, there was nothing that Buck would not do. One day after they had left Dawson for the headwaters of the Tanana, the men and dogs were resting on the edge of a cliff. The cliff fell away, straight down, to naked bedrock three hundred feet below. John Thornton was sitting near the edge, Buck at his shoulder. A thoughtless impulse seized Thornton, and he drew the attention of Hans and Pete to the experiment he had in mind. "Jump, Buck!" he commanded, sweeping his arm out and over the canyon. The next instant he was wrestling with Buck on the extreme edge of the cliff, while Hans and Pete were dragging them back to safety.

"It's spooky," Pete said, after it was over and they had caught their breath.

Thornton shook his head. "No, it is splendid, and

it is terrible, too. Do you know, it sometimes makes me afraid."

"I'm not eager to be the man that lays hands on you when he's around," Pete announced, nodding his head toward Buck.

"By Jingo!" Hans offered. "Not myself either."

It was at Circle City, before the year was out, that Pete's fears were realized. "Black" Burton, an evil-tempered and cruel man, had picked a quarrel with a tenderfoot at the bar. Thornton stepped good-naturedly between them. Buck, as was his custom, was lying in a corner, head on paws, watching his master's every action. Burton punched Thornton, without warning, straight from the shoulder. Thornton was sent spinning. He saved himself from falling only by grabbing the railing of the bar.

People in the bar heard what was neither a bark nor a yelp, but something that was best described as a roar. They saw Buck's body rise up in the air as he went straight for Burton's throat. The man saved his life by throwing his arm out, but he was knocked backward onto the floor, with Buck on top of him. Buck let go of his bite on the arm and drove in again for the man's throat. This time the man only partly blocked him, and his throat was torn open. Then the crowd drove Buck off, and a surgeon stopped the bleeding. Buck prowled up and down, growling furiously, trying to rush in, and being forced back by a number of men with clubs. A "miners' meeting," called on the spot, decided that the dog had enough cause for the attack, and Buck was let go. But his reputation was made, and from that day his name spread through every camp in Alaska.

Later on, in the fall of the year, he saved John

Thornton's life in a quite different way. The three partners were taking a long and narrow boat down a bad stretch of rapids on Forty Mile Creek. Hans and Pete walked along the bank, moving the boat by means of a rope that they tied from tree to tree. Thornton remained in the boat, helping it forward by means of a pole, and shouting directions to the men on the shore. Buck, on the bank, kept abreast of the boat. Worried and anxious, he never took his eyes off his master.

At a particularly bad spot, where a ledge of barely submerged rocks jutted out into the river, Hans untied the rope. While Thornton poled the boat out into the stream, Hans ran down the bank with the end of the rope, to tie the boat when it had cleared the ledge. The boat cleared the ledge and was flying swiftly downstream when Hans, trying to slow it down, pulled too sharply on the cord. The boat tipped over and hit the bank bottom up. Thornton was thrown out of the boat. He was carried downstream toward the worst part of the rapids, a stretch of wild water in which no swimmer could live.

Buck sprang into the water the instant the boat overturned. After three hundred yards, in the middle of a mad swirl of water, he caught up to Thornton. When he felt Thornton grasp his tail, Buck headed for the bank, swimming with all his splendid strength. But their progress toward the shore was slow, while their progress downstream was amazingly rapid. From below came the fatal roar where the wild current went wilder, hitting the rocks which thrust through like the teeth of an enormous comb. The pull of the water at the beginning of the last steep incline was horrendous. Thornton knew that it was impossible to make the shore. He scraped furiously over two rocks, then struck a third with crushing force. He grabbed its slippery top with both hands, releasing Buck. Above the roar of the churning water, he shouted, "Go, Buck! Go!"

Buck swept on downstream, struggling desperately. When he heard Thornton's command, he reared out of the water, throwing his head high as though for a last look. Then he turned obediently toward the bank. He swam powerfully. Pete and Hans dragged him ashore at the very point where swimming became impossible and destruction began.

They knew that a man could cling to a slippery rock in the face of the driving current for only a few minutes. They ran as fast as they could up the bank to a place far above where Thornton was hanging on. They attached the rope to Buck's neck and shoulders, being careful that it did not strangle him or get in the way of his swimming. Then they launched him into the stream. He swam boldly, but not straight enough into the stream. He discovered the mistake too late, when he missed Thornton by a few feet away and was carried helplessly past.

Hans pulled on the rope, as though Buck were a boat. Buck was pulled beneath the surface of the water, and he stayed there until his body hit the bank and he was pulled out. He was half drowned. Hans and Pete threw themselves on him, pounding the breath into him and the water out. Buck staggered to his feet and fell down. Thornton's voice came to them faintly, and although they could not make out the words, they could tell that his strength was almost gone. His master's voice acted on Buck like an electric shock. He sprang to his feet and ran up the bank to where he had jumped in before.

Again the rope was attached and he was launched. This time Buck swam straight into the stream. He had misjudged once, but he would not be guilty of it a second time. Buck held on until he was straight above Thornton. Then he turned and, with the speed of an express train, headed down toward him. Thornton saw him coming. As Buck struck him like a battering ram, with the whole force of the current behind him, he reached up and closed both arms around the shaggy neck. Hans tied the rope to a tree, and Buck and Thornton were jerked under the water. Strangling, suffocating, sometimes one on top and sometimes the other, dragging over the jagged bottom, smashing against rocks and snags, they were pulled in to the bank.

Thornton came to, face down. He was being pushed violently back and forth across a log by Hans and Pete. His first thought was for Buck. Night was howling over Buck's limp and apparently lifeless body, while Skeet was licking the wet face and closed eyes. When Buck came to, Thornton felt carefully over his body, finding three broken ribs.

"That settles it," he announced. "We camp right here." And camp they did, until Buck's ribs knitted and he was able to travel.

That winter, at Dawson, Buck performed another feat. This feat was not so heroic. On the totem pole of Alaskan fame, however, it put his name many notches higher. This feat particularly pleased the three men, for they needed the money to outfit themselves. They had wanted for a long time to go to the virgin East, where no other miners had yet gone. It happened because of a conversation in the Eldorado

Saloon. Men were bragging about their favorite dogs. One man said that his dog could start a sled with five hundred pounds and pull it away. A second man bragged six hundred for his dog. A third bragged seven hundred.

"Pooh! Pooh!" said John Thornton. "Buck can start a thousand pounds."

"And break it out? And pull it for a hundred yards?" demanded Matthewson, the man who had claimed seven hundred for his dog.

"And break it out, and pull it for a hundred yards," John Thornton said coolly.

"Well," Matthewson said, slowly and deliberately, so that all could hear, "I've got a thousand dollars that says he can't. And there it is." So saying, he slammed a bag of gold dust the size of a bologna sausage down on the bar.

Nobody spoke. Thornton's bluff had been called, if it was a bluff. He could feel a flush of warm blood creeping up his face. He did not know whether Buck could start a thousand pounds. Half a ton! The huge size of it shocked him. He had great faith in Buck's strength, and he had often thought that Buck could start such a load. But he had never faced the possibility of it. A dozen men were watching him, silent and waiting. Besides, he did not have a thousand dollars, nor did Hans or Pete.

"I've got a sled standing outside now, with twenty 50-pound sacks of flour on it," Matthewson went on. "So don't let that stop you."

Thornton did not reply. He did not know what to say. He glanced from face to face, in the absent-minded way of a man who has forgotten how to think and is looking for something to get himself started again.

The face of Jim O'Brien, an old-time friend, caught his eye. The face seemed to rouse him to do what he would never have dreamed of doing.

"Can you lend me a thousand?" he asked, almost in a whisper.

"Sure," answered O'Brien, thumping down an overflowing sack by the side of Matthewson's. "Though it's little faith I'm having, John, that the beast can do the trick."

The Eldorado emptied its occupants into the street to see the test. The tables were deserted, and the dealers and gamekeepers came out to see the outcome of the bet. Several hundred men, in furs and mittens, gathered near the sled. Matthewson's sled, loaded with a thousand pounds of flour, had been standing for a couple of hours. In the intense cold (it was sixty below zero), the runners had frozen fast to the hard-packed snow. Men offered odds of two to one that Buck could not budge the sled. A disagreement arose concerning the phrase "break out." O'Brien argued that Thornton should knock the runners loose, leaving it to Buck to "break it out" from a dead standstill. Matthewson argued that Buck had to break the runners from the frozen grip of the snow. A majority of the men decided in Matthewson's favor, and the odds went up to three to one against Buck.

There were no takers, even at those odds. No one believed that Buck could do it. Thornton had been hurried into the bet, heavy with doubt. Now, as he looked at the sled itself, with the regular team of ten dogs curled up in the snow in front of it, the task appeared even more impossible. Matthewson grew happier and happier.

"Three to one!" he announced. "I'll bet you another thousand at those odds, Thornton. What do you say?"

Thornton's doubt showed in his face, but his fighting spirit was aroused. It was the spirit that soars above odds, that does not recognize the impossible, and hears only the call to battle. He called Hans and Pete to come to him. Their sacks were slim. With Thornton's own, the three partners could rake together only two hundred dollars. This was their total capital. Yet they laid it without delay against Matthewson's six hundred.

The team of ten dogs was unhitched. Buck, with his own harness, was put into the sled. He sensed the excitement, and he felt that in some way he must do a great thing for John Thornton. There were whispers of admiration at how wonderful he looked. He was in perfect condition, without an extra ounce of flesh. The 150 pounds that he weighed were so many pounds of grit and power. His fur shone like silk. His mane, which ran down the neck and across the shoulders, seemed half bristled, at rest though it was. It seemed to lift with every movement, as though extra energy made each particular hair alive and active. The great chest and heavy front legs were in proportion with the rest of his body, and the muscles showed tightly beneath the skin. Men felt these muscles and said they were hard as iron, and the odds went down to two to one.

"Gad, sir! Gad, sir!" stuttered a man. "I offer you eight hundred for him, sir, before the test, sir. Eight hundred just as he stands."

Thornton shook his head and stepped to Buck's side.

"You must stand away from him," Matthewson protested. "Free play and plenty of room."

The crowd fell silent. The only voices were gamblers offering two to one, without any takers. Everyone agreed that Buck was a magnificent animal. But those twenty 50-pound sacks of flour kept them from betting on him.

Thornton knelt down by Buck's side. He took his head in his two hands and rested cheek to cheek. He did not playfully shake him, as he usually did, or murmur soft love curses. Instead, he whispered in his ear. "As you love me, Buck. As you love me," was what he whispered. Buck whined with quiet eagerness.

The crowd was watching with interest. Things were getting mysterious. It seemed like a magic spell of some kind. As Thornton got to his feet, Buck seized his mittened hand between his paws. He pressed in with his teeth. Then he let go, slowly, half unwillingly. It was the answer, given not in terms of speech but in terms of love. Thornton stepped well back.

"Now, Buck," he said.

Buck tightened the traces. Then he let them go slack by several inches. It was the way he had learned.

"Gee!" Thornton's voice rang out, sharp in the tense silence.

Buck swung to the right, ending with a plunge that took up the slack. His one hundred and fifty pounds stopped with a sudden jerk. The load shook, and under the runners there was a crisp crackling sound.

"Haw!" Thornton commanded.

Buck repeated the movement, this time to the left. The crackling sound became a snapping one as the sled turned several inches to the side. The sled was broken out. Men were holding their breaths, completely unaware that they were doing so.

"Now, MUSH!"

Thornton's command cracked out like a pistol shot. Buck threw himself forward, tightening the traces with a lunge. His whole body was gathered together in the tremendous effort, the muscles twisting and knotting like live things beneath the silky fur. His great chest was low to the ground, his head forward and down. His feet were flying like mad, the claws scarring the hard-packed snow. The sled swayed and trembled. One of his feet slipped, and a man groaned aloud. Then the sled lurched ahead in what looked like a quick series of jerks, though it never really came to a stop . . . half an inch . . . an inch . . . two inches. . . . The jerks grew less as the sled gained momentum, until it was moving steadily along.

Men gasped and began to breathe again, unaware that for a moment they had stopped breathing. Thornton was running behind, encouraging Buck with short, cheerful words. The distance had been measured off. As he neared the pile of firewood that marked the end of the hundred yards, a cheer began to grow and grow. It broke into a roar as he passed the firewood and halted on command. Every man was tearing himself loose, even Matthewson. Hats and mittens were flying in the air. Men were shaking hands, it did not matter with whom, and bubbling over in a general confusion.

But Thornton fell on his knees beside Buck.

Head was against head, and he was shaking him back and forth. Those who hurried up heard him cursing Buck, softly and lovingly.

"Gad, sir! Gad, sir!" sputtered the man who had spoken before. "I'll give you a thousand for him, sir, a thousand—twelve hundred, sir."

Thornton rose to his feet. His eyes were wet. The tears were streaming openly down his cheeks. "Sir," he said, "no, sir. You can go to hell, sir. It's the best I can do for you, sir."

Buck seized Thornton's hand in his teeth. Thornton shook him back and forth. The onlookers drew back to a respectful distance, as though all inspired by the same idea. They were polite enough not to interrupt again.

7 The Sounding of the Call

Buck earned sixteen hundred dollars in five minutes for John Thornton. This money made it possible for Thornton to pay off his debts and to journey with his partners into the East. They were searching for a fabled lost mine, the history of which was as old as the history of the country. Many men had looked for it. But few had found it, and more than a few had never returned from the search. This lost mine was steeped in tragedy and mystery. No one knew who the first man there had been. Even the oldest tradition knew nothing of him. From the beginning, there had been an old, run-down cabin. Dying men had sworn that both the cabin and the mine were there. As proof, they showed nuggets that were unlike any known grade of gold in the Northland.

But no living man had worked this mine. Wherefore John Thornton and Pete and Hans, with Buck and half a dozen other dogs, headed into the East on an unknown trail. They hoped to succeed where other men and dogs as good as themselves had failed. They sledded seventy miles up the Yukon, swung to the left into the Stewart River, passed the Mayo and the McQuestion, and held on until the Stewart itself became a little stream among the high mountains of the Continental Divide.

John Thornton was unafraid of the wild. With a

handful of salt and a rifle, he could plunge into the wilderness and get along wherever he pleased, and for as long a time as he pleased. He hunted his dinner during the day's travel. If he did not find a dinner, he would keep on traveling, sure that sooner or later he would come to it. So, on this great journey into the east, nothing but meat was on the menu. The sled was loaded mainly with ammunition and tools. They did not travel according to any schedule.

To Buck it was unending delight, this hunting, fishing, and wandering through strange places. For weeks at a time they would go on steadily, day after day. And for weeks on end they would camp. While the dogs loafed, the men would burn holes through the frozen mud and gravel, and wash countless pans of dirt by the heat of the fire. Sometimes they went hungry. Sometimes they feasted noisily. It all depended on how much game there was and their luck in hunting it. Summer came. Dogs and men backpacked, rafted across blue mountain lakes, and traveled along unknown rivers in slender boats made from the forest.

The months came and went. Back and forth they crossed through the wilderness, where there were no men, and yet where men had once been if the Lost Cabin were true. They went across divides in summer snowstorms. They shivered under the midnight sun on naked mountains between the timber line and the eternal snows. They dropped into summer valleys amid swarms of gnats and flies. In the shadows of glaciers, they picked strawberries and flowers as ripe and pretty as any in the Southland. In the fall of the year, they entered a weird lake country, sad and silent. Birds had been there once, but now there was no sign of life. There was only the blowing of chill winds, the forming of ice in sheltered places, and the quiet, sad splashing of waves on the lonely beaches.

They wandered through another winter, on the erased trails of men who had gone before. Once they came on a path blazed through the forest. It was an ancient path, and the Lost Cabin seemed very near. But the path began nowhere and ended nowhere, and it remained a mystery. Another time they found the wreckage of a hunting lodge. Amid the shreds of rotted blankets, John Thornton found a long-barreled flintlock. He recognized it as a Hudson Bay Company gun of the young days in the Northwest, when such a gun was worth its height in piled-up beaver skins. But there was no hint as to who had built the lodge or left the gun amid the blankets.

Spring came on once more. At the end of all their wandering they found, not the Lost Cabin, but a shallow sand bed where the gold showed like yellow butter across the bottom of the washing pan. They looked no farther. Each day of work earned them thousands of dollars in gold dust and nuggets, and they worked every day. The gold was sacked in moose-hide bags, fifty pounds to the bag, and piled like firewood outside the lodge. They worked like giants, the days following each other like dreams as they heaped the treasure up.

There was nothing for the dogs to do, except now and then hauling in meat that Thornton killed. Buck spent long hours musing by the fire. Now that there was little work to be done, the vision of the short-legged, hairy man came to him more and more often. Often, blinking by the fire, Buck wandered with him in that other world which he remembered.

The chief feature of this other world seemed to be fear. Buck watched the hairy man sleeping by the fire, his head between his knees and his hands clasped above. Buck saw that the man slept restlessly, with many twitches and awakenings. At such times, he would look fearfully into the darkness and throw more wood on the fire. Sometimes they walked along a beach, where the hairy man gathered shellfish, and ate them as he gathered. Then the man would look everywhere for hidden danger, and he would be prepared to run like the wind when it appeared. Sometimes they crept noiselessly through the forest, with Buck at the hairy man's heels. Both of them were alert and watchful, for the man heard and smelled as sharply as Buck. The hairy man could spring up into the trees and travel ahead as fast as on the ground. He swung by the arms from limb to limb, letting go and catching, never falling, never missing his grip. In fact, he seemed as much at home in the trees as on the ground. Buck had memories of nights spent guarding a tree, while the hairy man roosted above, holding on tightly as he slept.

And closely related to the visions of the hairy man was the call that still sounded in the depths of the forest. It filled him with great unrest and strange desires. He was aware of wild longings and stirrings for he knew not what. Sometimes he followed the call into the forest, looking for it as though it were something he could touch. He would bark, softly or defiantly depending on his mood. He would poke his nose into the cool wood moss, or into the black soil where long grasses grew, and snort with joy at the fat earth smells. Or he would crouch for hours, as if in hiding, behind fungus-covered trunks of fallen trees, wide-eyed and wide-eared to all that moved and sounded about him. It might be that, lying in this way, he hoped to capture this call that he could not understand. But he did not know why he did these things. He was driven to do them, and did not reason about them at all.

Overpowering urges took hold of him. He would be lying in camp, dozing lazily in the heat of day, when suddenly his head would lift and his ears cock up, listening intently. He would spring to his feet and dash away, and on and on, for hours, through the forest aisles and across the open spaces. He loved to run down dry creek beds, and to creep and spy on the bird life in the woods. For a day at a time he would lie in the underbrush where he could watch the partridges beating their wings and strutting up and down. But he especially loved to run in the dim twilight of the summer midnights. He listened to the quiet, sleepy murmurs of the forest, reading signs and sounds as a man may read a book. And at all times he followed after the mysterious something that called, waking or sleeping, for him to come.

One night he sprang from sleep with a start, eager-eyed, nostrils scenting, his mane bristling. From the forest came the call (or one note of it, for the call was many-noted), clear and definite as never before. It was a long, drawn howl, like the noise made by a husky dog, and at the same time not like it. And Buck knew it, in the old, familiar way, as a sound that he had heard before. He sprang from the sleeping camp and in swift silence dashed through the woods. As he grew closer to the cry, he went more slowly, with caution in every movement, until he came to an open place among the trees. Looking out, he saw a long, lean timber wolf, sitting up straight, with his nose pointed to the sky.

Buck had made no noise. Yet the wolf stopped its howling and tried to sense his presence. Buck moved cautiously into the open, half-crouching, body gathered compactly together, tail straight and stiff, feet falling with unusual care. Every movement advertised a mixture of danger and friendliness. It was the threatening truce that marks the meeting of wild animals. But the wolf ran off as soon as it saw him. Buck followed, leaping wildly, in frantic eagerness to catch up. He ran him into a blind channel, in the bed of a creek, where some fallen logs barred the way. The wolf whirled about, turning on his hind legs in the same way as Joe and of all cornered husky dogs. He was snarling and bristling, clicking his teeth together in a rapid, unbroken series of snaps.

Buck did not attack. Instead, he circled about him with friendly advances. The wolf was suspicious and afraid. Buck weighed three times as much as the wolf, and his head barely reached Buck's shoulder. Watching his chance, he ran quickly away, and the chase began again. Time and again he was cornered, and the thing repeated. The wolf was in poor condition, or Buck could not have caught up with him so easily. He would run until Buck's head was even with his side, when he would whirl around to protect himself, only to run away again at the first chance.

But in the end, Buck's stubbornness was rewarded. The wolf, finding that no harm was meant, finally sniffed noses with him. Then they became friendly and played in the nervous, partly shy way with which fierce animals pretend not to be fierce. After some time of this, the wolf started off at an easy walk that plainly showed he was going somewhere. He made it clear that he wanted Buck to come with him. They ran side by side through the dull, gloomy twilight, straight up the creek bed, into a gorge, and across the bleak divide where the creek began.

On the opposite slope, they came down into a level country with great stretches of forest and many streams. Through these great stretches they ran steadily, hour after hour, as the sun rose higher and the day grew warmer. Buck was wildly glad. He knew he was at last answering the call, running by the side of his wood brother toward the place from which the call surely came. Old memories were coming to him fast, and he was excited by them in the same way that he had once been excited by the real things of which these memories were the shadows. He had done this thing before, somewhere in that other, dimly remembered world. He was doing it again now, running free in the open, the unpacked earth underfoot, the wide sky overhead.

They stopped by a running stream to drink and, stopping, Buck remembered John Thornton. He sat down. The wolf started on toward the place from where the call surely came. Then he returned to Buck, sniffing noses and acting as if to encourage him. But Buck turned about and started slowly on the return track. For the better part of an hour, the wild brother ran by his side, whining softly. Then he sat down, pointed his nose upward, and howled. It was a mournful howl, and as Buck kept steadily on his way, he heard it grow faint and fainter until it was lost in the distance.

John Thornton was eating dinner when Buck dashed into camp and jumped on him in a frenzy of affection, knocking him down, jumping on him, licking his face, biting his hand. John Thornton described it as "playing the general tomfool," at the same time shaking Buck back and forth and cursing him lovingly.

For two days and nights Buck never left camp, never let Thornton out of his sight. He followed him around at his work, watched him while he ate, saw him into his blankets at night and out of them in the morning. But after two days, the call in the forest began to sound more strongly than ever. Buck's restlessness came back to him. He was haunted by memories of the wild brother, and of the smiling land beyond the divide, and of the run side by side through the wide forest stretches. Once again he began wandering in the woods, but the wild brother did not return. And though Buck listened through long nights, he never heard the mournful howl.

He began to sleep out at night, staying away from camp for days at a time. Once he crossed the divide at the head of the creek and went down into the land of timber and streams. He wandered there for a week, looking unsuccessfully for signs of the wild brother. He killed his meat as he traveled, and he moved with the long, easy lope that seemed never to grow tired. He fished for salmon in a broad stream that emptied somewhere into the sea. By this same stream he killed a large black bear, which had been blinded by mosquitoes while fishing and raged helplessly through the forest. Even so, it was a hard fight, and it brought out the last unused fierce part of Buck's nature. Two days later, he returned to his kill and found a dozen wolverines quarreling over it. He scattered them like chaff, and the ones that got away left two behind who would never quarrel again.

The longing for blood became stronger than ever before. He was a killer, a thing that preyed, living on the things that lived. He lived alone, without help, depending on his own strength and mastery. He survived and succeeded in an unfriendly environment where only the strong survived. Because of all this, he developed a great pride in himself, which showed in his appearance. It showed in all his movements, in the play of every muscle, in the way he carried himself. It made his glorious furry coat even more glorious. Except for the stray brown on his muzzle and above his eyes, and for the splash of white in the middle of his chest, he might have been mistaken for a gigantic wolf, larger than the largest of the breed. From his St. Bernard father he had inherited size and weight, but he was shaped like his shepherd mother. His muzzle was the long wolf muzzle, except that it was larger than the muzzle of any wolf. His head, somewhat broader, was the wolf head on a massive scale.

His cunning was wolf cunning, and wild cunning. His intelligence was shepherd intelligence and St. Bernard intelligence. All of this, plus experience gained in the fiercest of schools, made him as awesome a creature as any that ever roamed the wild. Living on a straight meat diet, he was in full flower, at the high tide of his life, overflowing with vigor and vitality. When Thornton passed his hand along Buck's back, a snapping and crackling followed the hand as each hair let go its built-up magnetism.

Every part, brain and body, nerve tissue and fiber, was tuned to the most perfect pitch, and between all the parts there was a perfect balance. When action was needed, he responded as quickly as lightning. As quick as a husky dog was to attack or defend, Buck was twice as fast. He saw a movement, or heard a sound, and responded while another dog would still have been listening. His muscles were charged with vitality, and snapped into play sharply, like steel springs. Life streamed through him in a splendid flood, until it seemed that he would explode with joy.

"Never was there such a dog," said John Thornton one day, as the partners watched Buck marching out of camp.

"When he was made, the mold was broke," said Pete.

"By jingo! I think so myself," said Hans.

They saw him marching out of camp. But they did not see the instant and terrible change that took place in him as soon as he entered the forest. He no longer marched. He became a thing of the wild, stealing along softly, cat-footed, a passing shadow that appeared and disappeared among the shadows. He knew how to take advantage of every hiding place, how to crawl on his belly like a snake, and how like a snake to leap and strike. He could take a bird from its nest, kill a rabbit as it slept, and snap the little chipmunks in midair. Fish, in open pools, were not quick enough to escape him. He caught beaver mending their dams, no matter how careful they were. He killed to eat, not from cruelty. But he preferred to eat what he killed himself. So a hidden humor ran through his actions. He liked to steal up on squirrels and, when he had almost caught them, to let them go, chattering in deathly fear.

As the fall of the year came on, the moose appeared in larger numbers, moving slowly down to spend the winter in the lower and less harsh valleys. Buck had already dragged down a stray part-grown calf. But he wished strongly for larger and more difficult game, and he came upon it one day on the divide at the head of the creek. A band of twenty moose had crossed over from the land of streams and timber, and chief among them was a great bull. He was in a savage temper. Standing over six feet from the ground, he was as tough an enemy as even Buck could wish for. Back and forth the bull tossed his great antlers, which branched to fourteen points and were seven feet from tip to tip. His small eyes burned with a vicious and bitter light, while he roared with fury at the sight of Buck.

A feathered arrow end stuck out from his side, which accounted for his savageness. Guided by the instinct from the old hunting days of the primitive world, Buck proceeded to cut the bull off from the herd. It was not an easy task. He would bark and dance about in front of the bull, just out of reach of the great antlers and the terrible hoofs, which could have stamped his life out in a single blow. Unable to turn his back on Buck and go away, the bull was driven into fits of rage. Then he charged Buck, who retreated shrewdly, luring him on by pretending to be unable to escape. But when the Buck was separated in this way from the rest of the moose, two or three of the younger bulls would charge Buck, and enable the wounded bull to rejoin the herd.

There is a patience of the wild that is dogged,

tireless, persistent as life itself. It is the patience that holds the spider in its web motionless for endless hours, and the snake in its coils, and the panther in its hiding place. This patience belongs in particular to life when it hunts its living food. And it belonged to Buck as he clung to the herd, slowing its march, irritating the young bulls, worrying the cows with their half-grown calves, and driving the wounded bull mad with helpless rage. For half a day this continued. Buck attacked from all sides, surrounding the herd with a whirlwind of danger, cutting out his victim as soon as it rejoined the herd. He wore out the patience of his victims, which is not as great a patience as that of the hunter.

As the day wore along and the sun dropped to its bed in the northwest (the darkness had come back, and the nights were six hours long), the young bulls were more and more unwilling to come to the aid of their leader. It seemed that they could never shake off this single-minded creature that held them back. Besides, it was not the life of the herd that was threatened, or the lives of the young bulls. The life of only one member was demanded, which was not so close to their own lives. In the end, they were willing to pay the price.

As twilight fell, the old bull stood with lowered head, watching his herd—the cows he had known, the calves he had fathered, the bulls he had mastered—as they plodded on through the fading light. He could not follow, for the merciless fanged terror that would not let him go leaped up in front of his nose. He weighed more that 1,300 pounds. He had lived a long, strong life, full of fight and struggle. At the end, he faced death at the teeth of a creature whose head did not reach above his great knuckled knees.

From then on, night and day, Buck never left his prey. He never gave it a moment's rest, never allowed it to eat the leaves of trees or the shoots of birch and willow. Nor did he give the wounded bull a chance to satisfy his burning thirst in the slender trickling streams they crossed. Often, in desperation, the bull burst into long stretches of running. At such times, Buck did not try to stop him, but loped easily at his heels. He was satisfied with the way the game was being played. He would lie down when the moose stood still, and attack him fiercely when he tried to eat or drink.

The great head drooped more and more under its tree of antlers, and the trot grew weak and weaker. He took to standing for long periods, with nose to the ground and sad ears drooping limply. Buck found more time to get water for himself and to rest. At such times, panting with red tongue, and with eyes fixed on the bull, it seemed to Buck that a change was coming. He could feel a new stir in the land. As the moose were coming into the land, so other kinds of life were also coming in. Forest and stream and air seemed alive with their presence. The news of it did not reach him by sight or sound or smell, but by some other sense. He heard nothing, saw nothing. Yet he knew that the land was somehow different, that strange things were in it. He decided to look into it after he had finished the business in hand.

At last, at the end of the fourth day, he pulled the great moose down. For a day and a night he remained by the kill, eating and sleeping. Then, rested and strong, he turned his face toward camp and

John Thornton. He broke into the long, easy lope, and went on, hour after hour, always sure of the way. Heading straight home through strange country, he had a sureness of direction that put man and his compass to shame.

As he went along, he became more and more aware of the new stir in the land. There was life in it different from the life that had been there throughout the summer. No longer did this fact come to him in some mysterious way. The birds talked about it, the squirrels chattered about it, the breezes whispered of it. Several times he stopped and drew in the fresh morning air in great sniffs, reading a message which made him leap on with greater speed. He was weighed down with a sense that a disaster was happening, or perhaps had already happened. As he crossed the last watershed and dropped down into the valley toward camp, he proceeded with greater caution.

Three miles away, he came upon a fresh trail that sent his neck hair rippling and bristling. It led straight toward camp and John Thornton. Buck hurried on, swiftly but cautiously, every nerve straining and tense. He took in all of the many details that told a story—all but the end of it. His nose told him much about the creatures who had traveled there just before him. He noticed the silence of the forest. The bird life had flown away. The squirrels were in hiding. He saw only one, a sleek, gray fellow flattened against a gray, dead limb, so that he seemed a part of it.

As Buck slid along like a gliding shadow, his nose was jerked suddenly to the side as though a force had pulled it. He followed the new scent into a thicket and found Night. He was lying on his side, dead where he had dragged himself. An arrow, head and feathers, stuck out from both sides of his body.

A hundred yards farther on, Buck came upon one of the sled dogs Thornton had bought in Dawson. This dog was thrashing about in a death struggle, directly on the trail. Buck passed around him without stopping. From the camp came the faint sound of many voices, rising and falling in a singsong chant. Edging forward to the edge of the clearing, Buck found Hans, lying on his face, stuck full of arrows like a porcupine. At the same instant, Buck peered out where the lodge had been. What he saw made his hair leap straight up on his neck and shoulders. A strong rush of overpowering rage swept over him. He did not know that he growled, but he growled fiercely. For the last time in his life, he allowed emotion to overcome reason. It was because of his great love for John Thornton that he lost his head.

The Yeehats were dancing about the wreckage of the lodge when they heard a fearful roaring. They saw an animal rushing upon them like none they had ever seen before. It was Buck, a live hurricane of fury, throwing himself on them in a frenzy to destroy. He sprang at the man in front (it was the chief of the Yeehats), ripping his throat wide open until the torn jugular spouted a fountain of blood. He did not pause over the victim, but with the next bound tore wide the throat of a second man. There was no way to resist him. He plunged among them, tearing, destroying, in constant and terrific motion. His movements were so fast, and the Indians were so close together, that they shot one another with their arrows, instead of hitting Buck. One young hunter, throwing a spear at Buck, drove it through the chest of another hunter with such force that it came out his back. Then a panic seized the Yeehats, and they fled in terror to the woods, announcing as they fled the coming of the Evil Spirit.

And Buck was truly the Devil in the body of a dog. He raged at their heels and dragged them down like deer as they raced through the trees. It was a disastrous day for the Yeehats. They scattered far and wide over the country. It was not until a week later that the last of the survivors gathered together in a lower valley and counted their losses. As for Buck, he grew tired of the pursuit and returned to the ruined camp. He found Pete where he had been killed in his blankets in the first moment of surprise. Thornton's desperate struggle left a trail of fresh scents in the ground, and Buck scented every detail of it down to the edge of a deep pool. By the edge, head and front feet in the water, lay Skeet, faithful to the last. The pool itself, muddy and discolored from the gold mining, hid what it contained. And it contained John Thornton, for Buck followed his trace into the water, and no trace led away.

All day Buck brooded by the pool or wandered restlessly around the camp. He knew what death was, and he knew John Thornton was dead. It left a great emptiness in him, somewhat like hunger, but an emptiness that ached and ached, and which food could not fill. At times, when he paused to look at the bodies of the Yeehats, he forgot the pain of it. At such times he was aware of a great pride in himself, a pride greater than any he had yet known. He had killed man, the noblest game of all, and he had killed in the face of the law of club and fang. He sniffed the bodies curiously. They had died so easily. It was harder to kill a husky dog than them. They were no match at all, were it not for their arrows and spears and clubs. From now on he would be unafraid of them except when they carried their arrows, spears, and clubs.

Night came on, and a full moon rose high over the trees into the sky, lighting the land until it lay bathed in ghostly day. And with the coming of the night, brooding and mourning by the pool, Buck became aware of a new life in the forest in addition to that of the Yeehats. He stood up, listening and scenting. From far away drifted a faint, sharp yelp, followed by a chorus of similar sharp yelps. As the moments passed, the yelps grew closer and louder. Again, Buck knew them as things heard in that other world of his memory. He walked to the center of the open space and listened. It was the call, the many-noted call, sounding more attractive and forceful than ever before. And as never before, he was ready to obey. John Thornton was dead. The last tie was broken. Man and the claims of man no longer bound him.

The wolves hunted their living meat as the Yeehats had hunted it, following the migrating moose. Following the moose, the wolf pack had at last crossed over from the land of streams and timber and invaded Buck's valley. Into the clearing where the moonlight streamed, they poured in a silvery flood. Buck stood in the center of the clearing, waiting for them, motionless as a statue. He stood so large and still that they were awed, and a moment's silence fell. Then the boldest one leaped straight for him. Like a flash Buck struck, breaking the neck.

Then he stood, without movement, as before, while the stricken wolf rolled in agony behind him. Three others tried it in quick order. One after the other they drew back, blood streaming from their slashed throats or shoulders.

This was enough to push the whole pack forward, crowded together, blocked and confused by its eagerness to pull down their prey. Buck's marvelous quickness and skill served him well. Turning on his hind legs, snapping and gnashing, he was everywhere at once. But to prevent them from getting behind him, he was forced back, down past the pool and into the creek bed, until he came up against a high gravel bank. He worked along to a right angle in the bank, which the men had made in the course of mining. In this angle he came to bay, protected on three sides and with nothing to do but face the front.

He faced it so well that, after half an hour, the wolves drew back uneasily. The tongues of all were out and lolling, the white fangs showing cruelly white in the moonlight. Some were lying down with heads raised and ears forward. Others stood on their feet, watching him. Still others were lapping water from the pool. One wolf, long and lean and gray, advanced cautiously, in a friendly manner. Buck recognized the wild brother with whom he had run for a night and a day. He was whining softly, and, as Buck whined, they touched noses.

Then an old wolf, gaunt and battle-scarred, came forward. Buck worked his lips into the beginning of a snarl, but sniffed noses with him. Then the old wolf sat down, pointed his nose at the moon, and broke out the long wolf howl. The others sat down and howled. And now the call came clearly to Buck.

He, too, sat down and howled. When he had finished, he came out of his angle, and the pack crowded around him, sniffing in a half-friendly, half-savage manner. The leaders sounded the yelp of the pack and sprang away into the woods. The wolves swung in behind, yelping in chorus. And Buck ran with them, side by side with the wild brother, yelping as he ran.

And here may well end the story of Buck. It was not many years before the Yeehats noticed a change in the breed of timber wolves. Some had splashes of brown on head and muzzle, with a patch of white centering down the chest. But more remarkable than this, the Yeehats tell of a Ghost Dog that runs at the head of the pack. They are afraid of this Ghost Dog, for it has cunning greater than they. It steals from their camps in fierce winters, robs their traps, slays their dogs, and challenges their bravest hunters.

And there is more to the story. There are hunters who fail to return to the camp. There have been hunters found by their tribesmen with throats slashed cruelly open, and with wolf prints about them in the snow greater than the prints of any wolf. Each fall, when the Yeehats follow the movement of the moose, there is a certain valley which they never enter. And there are women who become sad when it is told by the fire of how the Evil Spirit came to select that valley for a dwelling place.

In the summers there is one visitor, however, to that valley, of which the Yeehats do not know. It is a great, gloriously coated wolf, like, and yet not like, all the other wolves. He crosses alone from the smiling timber land and comes down upon an open space among the trees. Here a yellow stream flows from rotted moose-hide sacks and sinks into the ground. Long grasses grow through it, and vegetable mold runs over it and hides its yellow from the sun. Here he dreams for a time, howling once, long and mournfully, before he leaves.

But he is not always alone. When the long winter nights come on, and the wolves follow their meat into the lower valley, he may be seen running at the head of the pack. Through the pale moonlight or glimmering northern lights, he leaps like a giant above his fellows, his great throat singing the song of the younger world, which is the song of the pack.

REVIEWING YOUR READING

CHAPTER 1

FINDING THE MAIN IDEA
1. The most important thing that happens in this chapter is
(A) Buck travels on the *Narwhal*   (B) Buck is kidnapped
(C) Buck meets Curly   (D) Buck does not read

REMEMBERING DETAILS
2. This story takes place
(A) in the future   (B) in the year 1987   (C) in the year
1897   (D) hundreds of years ago
3. Perrault purchased Buck for
(A) fifty dollars   (B) one hundred fifty dollars
(C) three hundred dollars (D) gold
4. At Judge Miller's Place, Buck was
(A) a kennel dog (B) a house dog   (C) a watchdog
(D) a ranch pet
5. Manuel sold Buck to get money for
(A) his children (B) his gambling habit (C) Judge Miller
(D) gardening tools

DRAWING CONCLUSIONS
6. Strong dogs were in danger because
(A) they were being sold to men in the Klondike (B) an
illness was killing them (C) they were being tortured
(D) the weather was frigid
7. You can figure that François and Perrault
(A) will be reasonable masters   (B) will continue to be
cruel to Buck   (C) will return Buck to the ranch
(D) will give Buck a happy life

USING YOUR REASON
8. The "yellow metal" found in the Arctic darkness was
(A) money   (B) copper   (C) gold   (D) jewelry

IDENTIFYING THE MOOD
9. In this chapter, the author has created a feeling of
(A) calm   (B) horror   (C) suspense   (D) excitement

114

1. What do you think was behind Buck's ferocious rage toward his kidnappers? Do you think that it was his wounded pride or his basic nature? Explain.

CHAPTER 2

FINDING THE MAIN IDEA
1. The main purpose of this chapter is to
   (A) show what life will be like for Buck in the Northland
   (B) describe the Northland setting   (C) describe Curly's brutal death   (D) show how Buck had changed

REMEMBERING DETAILS
2. Which dog had the lead position on the team?
   (A) Dave   (B) Sol-leks   (C) Buck   (D) Spitz
3. While he worked, Buck suffered from
   (A) homesickness   (B) frostbite   (C) pangs of hunger
   (D) fatigue
4. Buck's position on the team was between Dave and Sol-leks so they could be his
   (A) friends   (B) protectors   (C) teachers   (D) students
5. The first law of club and fang that Buck learned was
   (A) wait your turn   (B) no fair play   (C) share
   (D) be friendly
6. Sleeping was difficult for Buck until he discovered the other dogs
   (A) were cuddled together   (B) were in the tent
   (C) were buried in holes under the snow   (D) had left camp

DRAWING CONCLUSIONS
7. Buck began to steal food from the other dogs
   (A) for fun   (B) in order to survive   (C) because he was greedy   (D) to tease Spitz
8. All of the words below describe Buck except for
   (A) reasonable   (B) observant   (C) reckless   (D) intelligent

USING YOUR REASON
9. Buck was able to adopt the ways of his ancestors because
   (A) Judge Miller taught them to him   (B) he inherited them   (C) he learned them from Perrault   (D) he watched Spitz

1. Explain "The Law of Club and Fang" in your own words. Include some examples from the chapter in your description.

CHAPTER 3

FINDING THE MAIN IDEA
1. This chapter is mostly about
   (A) the war between Buck and Spitz   (B) how the team survived on thin ice   (C) Perrault's strength and courage   (D) the invasion by wild dogs

REMEMBERING DETAILS
2. As a courier for the Canadian government, Perrault's job was to transport
   (A) gold   (B) men   (C) mail and supplies   (D) dogs
3. The team rested for seven days in
   (A) Dyea   (B) Lake Labarge   (C) Seattle   (D) Dawson
4. What did the team have to do when they reached the Thirty Mile River?
   (A) swim   (B) rest   (C) scale the cliffs   (D) wait for it to freeze over
5. Who saved Buck from Dolly after she went mad?
   (A) Spitz   (B) Perrault   (C) François   (D) Pike and Dub
6. The one quality that led to Buck's triumph over Spitz was
   (A) persistence   (B) loyalty   (C) strength   (D) imagination

DRAWING CONCLUSIONS
7. Buck began his quest for power over Spitz by
   (A) entering into Spitz's fights   (B) attacking Spitz directly   (C) attacking the other dogs   (D) stealing food
8. The quarrels between Buck and Spitz
   (A) made the team work harder   (B) made Perrault furious   (C) created disharmony in the team   (D) had no effect at all

USING YOUR REASON
9. François and Perrault were able to predict Spitz's defeat because
   (A) they liked Buck better   (B) Buck was bigger
   (C) Spitz was older   (D) they saw how quickly Buck had learned

IDENTIFYING THE MOOD

10. In this chapter, the author created a feeling of
    (A) calmness (B) excitement (C) mystery (D) sadness

THINKING IT OVER

1. What do you think the author's opinion of Buck was? What did he think of Spitz? Which dog did you like better? Give reasons to support your opinion.
2. In this chapter, the author compares man's joy of hunting and killing with an animal's "lust for blood." Do you think they are the same or are they different? Explain.

CHAPTER 4

FINDING THE MAIN IDEA

1. Another title for this chapter might be
   (A) "The Defeat" (B) "Sol-leks's Revenge"
   (C) "A Good Leader" (D) "Good-bye Dave"

REMEMBERING DETAILS

2. Which dog did François want to lead the team?
   (A) Buck (B) Sol-leks (C) Dave (D) Pike
3. Why did Buck think that he deserved the lead position on the team?
   (A) he was older (B) he was bigger (C) he had earned it (D) François had promised it
4. What kind of leader did Buck turn out to be?
   (A) a weak leader (B) too reckless (C) even better than Spitz (D) stubborn
5. The temperature during the entire trip was
   (A) 50 degrees (B) 15 degrees below zero (C) 50 degrees below zero (D) freezing
6. Which of the following did not take place for the team?
   (A) Buck became their leader (B) a Scot became the new driver (C) Dave died (D) they no longer carried mail

DRAWING CONCLUSIONS

7. You can assume that the Scot shot Dave
   (A) because he was no longer needed (B) to put him out of his misery (C) because he wasn't working hard enough (D) because he tried to abandon the team

8. You might conclude that a sled dog would rather die
(A) than suffer   (B) while working   (C) quickly
(D) alone

USING YOUR REASON
9. The hairy man Buck sees in his dream probably is
(A) Perrault   (B) Judge Miller   (C) a caveman
(D) the Scot

IDENTIFYING THE MOOD
10. When Dave died, the dogs were
(A) happy   (B) sad   (C) unconcerned   (D) angry

THINKING IT OVER
1. What does the statement, "Far more powerful were the memories inherited from his ancestors" tell you about Buck's adjustment to the primitive way of life? From this statement, can you predict how the story might end? Explain.

CHAPTER 5

FINDING THE MAIN IDEA
1. This chapter is mostly concerned with
(A) springtime in the Arctic   (B) the dangers of being inexperienced in the Arctic   (C) having enough food
(D) the search for gold

REMEMBERING DETAILS
2. In Skagway, Buck and the other dogs on the team
(A) rested   (B) prepared for another trip   (C) were replaced   (D) joined Perrault's team
3. Buck and the team were sold
(A) to the Canadian police   (B) to John Thornton
(C) to two men from the states   (D) for gold
4. Fourteen dogs are too many on a team because
(A) of their weight   (B) the dogs begin to fight
(C) it is too expensive   (D) the sled cannot carry enough food for them
5. The overloaded sled would not move at first because
(A) the dogs did not pull hard enough   (B) it was broken   (C) Hal was inexperienced   (D) the runners were frozen in the snow

6. Which dogs died first?
   (A) Dub and Buck (B) the Outside dogs (C) Billee and Teek (D) Buck and Sol-leks
7. How many dogs were left by the time they reached John Thornton's camp?
   (A) one (B) six (C) five (D) twelve
8. Who saved Buck?
   (A) Hal (B) John Thornton (C) Mercedes (D) Charles

DRAWING CONCLUSIONS
9. Buck would not move from Thornton's camp even when Hal whipped him because
   (A) he wanted to stay with Thornton (B) his feet were too sore (C) he knew the ice was thin and dangerous (D) he knew they were headed in the wrong direction
10. Rotten ice is
    (A) garbage-filled ice (B) dirty ice (C) melted ice (D) ice that weakens from underneath
11. Most of the trail between Skagway and Dawson was
    (A) over snow-covered mountains (B) between high cliffs (C) over frozen rivers and lakes (D) through the wilderness

THINKING IT OVER
1. Tell in your own words how the warmer spring weather can make the Arctic an extremely dangerous place. Include descriptions from the chapter in your explanation.
2. Why do you think the new drivers failed in the Arctic? Was it due to their civilized ways, their lack of experience, or something else? Explain your answer.
3. Why do you think John Thornton put his life on the line to save Buck?

CHAPTER 6

FINDING THE MAIN IDEA
1. This chapter is mostly about the friendship between
   (A) Thornton and Hans (B) Hans and Pete (C) Buck and Thornton (D) Skeet and Night

REMEMBERING DETAILS
2. Buck would bite John Thornton's hand to show his
   (A) anger (B) strength (C) love (D) power

3. The only thing that held Buck back from going into the wild was
   (A) his memory of Sol-leks   (B) his love for John Thornton   (C) his poor health   (D) his longing for the Southland
4. Hans and Pete worried about someone threatening
   (A) them   (B) Buck   (C) Thornton   (D) Skeet
5. Why did Buck attack the man in the bar?
   (A) he had punched Thornton   (B) he had kicked Buck   (C) he had started a fight   (D) he reminded him of Hal
6. Buck later saved Thornton from
   (A) starving   (B) freezing   (C) drowning   (D) the wild dogs
7. Buck proved his great strength and power by
   (A) pulling a thousand logs   (B) climbing the steep cliff   (C) pulling a thousand pounds of flour
   (D) pulling five hundred pounds of firewood

DRAWING CONCLUSIONS
8. Why do you think Buck was able to move the sled?
   (A) he was very strong   (B) he wanted to show his devotion to Thornton   (C) he knew how to break out the sled   (D) all of the above
9. Buck's main problem in this chapter is
   (A) his quick temper   (B) his longing for home
   (C) deciding between going into the forest and staying with Thornton   (D) getting along with Skeet and Night

USING YOUR REASON
10. What does Thornton represent to Buck?
   (A) civilization   (B) the wild   (C) happiness   (D) wealth

THINKING IT OVER
1. Why do you think Buck was so extremely loyal to Thornton? Was it because Thornton had saved him and was kind to him? Or, do you think Thornton reminded him of the civilized ways he had been forced to give up? Explain your answer.
2. How do you think this book will end? Do you think Buck will give in to the call of the wild that haunts him in this chapter? Explain your opinion.

120

CHAPTER 7

FINDING THE MAIN IDEA
1. In this chapter the author tells mainly about
   (A) the Yeehat Indians (B) how Buck killed a bull moose (C) Buck's urge to live in the wild (D) life with the pack

REMEMBERING DETAILS
2. How long did the trip take to the lost gold mine?
   (A) one season (B) one month (C) one week
   (D) one year
3. At first, what did Buck do while Thornton searched for gold?
   (A) he lay by the fire (B) he went into the forest
   (C) he hunted wolves (D) he hunted moose
4. The howl that came from the forest was made by
   (A) the wind (B) a lost sled dog (C) a wolf
   (D) a moose
5. What was the major change that took place in Buck?
   (A) his size (B) the thickness of his coat
   (C) his sleep habits (D) his thirst for blood
6. The one thing that allowed Buck to defeat the moose was his
   (A) size (B) cleverness (C) weight (D) patience
7. Who killed Thornton and his men?
   (A) wolves (B) gold seekers (C) Yeehat Indians
   (D) revenging moose

DRAWING CONCLUSIONS
8. Whose thoughts were revealed by the narrator of this story?
   (A) Thornton's (B) the Yeehats' (C) Buck's
   (D) the wolves'
9. In the end, the decision about whether or not to answer the call of the wild is made for Buck
   (A) when he defeats the moose (B) when he finds Thornton dead (C) when he hears the wolf howl
   (D) when they find gold

USING YOUR REASON

10. Where do you think Buck's visions of living at an earlier time came from?
    (A) Thornton whispered them to him   (B) the wolf described them   (C) he inherited them   (D) he imagined them
11. In this story, a sense of longing for a primitive time is
    (A) impossible to imagine   (B) the call of the wild
    (C) common among the Yeehats   (D) the call of the wolves

THINKING IT OVER

1. In what ways were Buck and John Thornton alike? Explain. Give at least two examples.
2. Do you think animals inherit traits of their ancient ancestors? If you were forced to live a primitive way of life, do you think you would begin to dream about the ways of ancient man? What might you dream about? Discuss your ideas.
3. Did the predictions made in the stories about the lost gold mine come true? How?